BOG ORCHIDS

Island Poems

Susan Deborah King

ISLAND INSTITUTE

Bog Orchids: Island Poems ©2010 by Susan Deborah King

Published by
Island Institute
386 Main Street
Rockland, ME 04841
www.islandinstitute.org

Cover photos by Geoffrey Wadsworth, Geoffworth@verizon.net
Book design & layout by Liz Tufte, Folio Bookworks
Author photo by Jim Gertmenian

ISBN: 978-0942719437

Printed in the U.S.A.

This book is dedicated with love
to the memory of these islanders:

Harry Alley
Edna Andrade
Trudy Bancroft
Wesley Bracey
Arthur Bunker
Tud Bunker
Lyn and Emily Colby
Bob Cumming
Bill Goldberg
Betty Hartley
Jack Heliker
Bob LaHotan
Bo Lea
Nancy Lea
Robert Mc Shea
Fred Moss
Hal Newell, Sr.
Hal Newell, Jr.
"Snooks" Peterson
Priscilla Richardson
Robin Richman
Emily Roberts
June Sampson
Norman Sanborn
Isabel and Stan Seimer
Stuart Silvers
David Stainton
Carl Strandberg
Andy Storey
Charles and Jean Wadsworth
Herbert Ware
Karl Wedge
Bea Weinreich
Betsy Wells

ACKNOWLEDGEMENTS

First and foremost, I want to thank the island and its residents for the inspiration and healing they have brought and continue to bring to my life. The island is the only place I have ever felt truly at home. It is not where I was born and raised, but it is where I feel I belong and am part of the community. I claim it as my natural habitat and native territory. Being in the matrix of this community has fostered my growth as a person and an artist. Here I have felt the support and safety I have needed to thrive. For this, my gratitude is immeasurable.

I thank the Island Institute for its work in promoting the continuance of viable human habitation of Maine islands and the preservation of the islands' natural beauty. My admiration of their mission and how they carry it out makes me particularly honored and pleased that they stand behind my work. In particular, I am grateful for David Tyler's help in shepherding this book into being.

I am very grateful, too, to Liz Tufte for the company of her spirit and for her artistic and practical expertise in creating a beautiful book design. Thanks, as well, to many friends for their constant encouragement and to my husband, Jim Gertmenian, my daughters, Emily and Enid, and my son-in-law, Brendan Callahan, for their love and forebearance.

CONTENTS

WHAT THE ISLAND SAID

I

I
3

TOURIST BOAT   5
CLOVER   6
UP WITH FISHERMEN AND BIRDS   7
CLOTHESLINE   8
BLACK LOCUST   9
SUN   11
EVERYDAY WONDERS: Oases for a Grief   12
NEIGHBORHOOD   13
NEW MOON   15
BUG BOY   16
BEE BALM   19
CROW ISLAND   20
SLIME MOLD   21
CAPRELLA MUTICA   22
RUDBECKIA   24
BEAUTY BUSH   25
MOSS   27
NOTE   28
LUPINE BLOOM   29
TWO   31
WEIRD THINGS IN MY NEIGHBORHOOD   33

ISLAND JOURNAL
35

II

49

OUR LADY OF NEVER MIND	51
ROCK	52
ROCKWEED	53
PUMP ELEGY	54
THE PEONIES	56
BENEFIT	57
OSPREY CRIES	58
RESURGENCE	59
RUTH ON HER PORCH	60
COMMUNITY	61
FRAMBOISE	63
WATERMELON	64
DEAD LOW	65
JAWLINE, STRONG	66
BOG ORCHIDS	67
FRENCHBORO	68
IN PRAISE OF FOG	69
NAMES OF BOATS	70
CAPTAIN DAN	72
CHANTERELLES	74
WHITE ELEPHANT	75
GRASSES	77
INSECT ENVY	79
PINK WATER	80
VANITAS	81
THREE LOBSTERS	82
TRACTOR	83

ISLAND JOURNAL
85

Fire	87
Blueberries	87
Sea Truck	88
Coyote	89
Memorials	89
Island Wedding	90
Quiet	91
Crocs	92
Blight	92
Cultural Center	93
Hermit Thrushes	94
Empty Houses	94
Storm Surf	95
Departure Prevention Committee	96

III
97

ISLAND GODDESS	99
FINBACK	100
MORNING	101
WILD CRANBERRIES	102
THE LAST	103
WALKING WITH BETSY	104
WINTERSPEAK	105
ELEGY FOR ROBIN	106
GHOST OVERWHELM	107
ROBIN	108
HELD, HEALING	109
JACK'S FACES	110
NEIGHBORS	112
REQUEST ON DANCING ROCKS	114
LARCHES	115

PLENILUNE, AUGUST 116

NIGHT OF ELEMENTS DISGUISED 117

THRUMCAP 118

DEADHEADING 119

SAX 120

WHERE HAS SUMMER GONE? 121

DARK HOUSES 123

SEPTEMBER LIGHT 124

MOONLESS NIGHTS 125

GREAT HEAD, DUSK, OCTOBER 126

ABOUT THE AUTHOR
129

I asked the earth, I asked the sea and the deeps,
among the living animals, the things that creep. I
asked the winds that blow, I asked the heavens, the
sun, the moon, the stars, and to all things that stand
at the doors to my flesh . . . my question was the gaze
I turned to them. Their answer was their beauty.

– St. Augustine

WHAT THE ISLAND SAID

Don't develop me,
for God's sake,
any further!
Heavy enough the houses
you've lain already on my back.
Don't sell pieces of me off
to bounders who say they find me beautiful –
why wouldn't they? –
but just want something on the side
and won't commit.
And *please*, let my bogs
stay boggy.
I like the rich, spongy muckinesss
of decay. It's the way
I build myself up,
layer by slowly contemplated layer.
Slow is how I like to do things,
but who pays me any heed?
I thought the spruces I grew
after sheep gnawed me raw
would be bristle enough
to fend off most comers.
I underestimated human vulgarity.
The way things are heating up,
in no time, I'll be sunk.
Until then, just let me
enjoy waves massaging my shores,
rattling my rocks, the wind
crooning through the needles of my trees
breezes brushing my grasses
a thousand strokes a night,
warblers' erotic envoys,
the boom and bust of storms
shaking me down
washing me,
for a time at least,
clean.

I

The sun has so much room to shine in there. It has
the whole sky to shine in, and it has miles and miles
of hills and woods, it has islands and rocks and boats
to glisten on and soak into like oil... There is no other
way to express my gratitude for all this, except to
burst into leaves and flowers.

— Katharine Butler Hathaway
The Little Locksmith

TOURIST BOAT

When they see it for the first time
as the ferry pulls out of the harbor:
Acadia's hand-carved-by-glaciers mountains,
the wide, cloud-embellished sky,
the islands like sea denizens emerging
from the wind-exhilerated deep, chatter about
tickets, schedules, the night life in Bar Harbor
                              stops. They fall silent.
They hook fingers into the net cradling
life jackets overhead and lean toward it,
cameras, binoculars swinging from their necks.
They put their day packs, their bike helmets
down on the bench, get up and move
from one side of the boat to the other
to confirm that they are utterly surrounded
by grandeur, engulfed in almost every hue of blue
cut by serrated, black-green horizontal strips,
the spruces. They point and murmur. Even
cranky, vacation-weary kids become, for moments,
rapt. As their tees and sweatshirts attest,
they come from all over: Michigan, Paris, Tokyo,
Dalton, Georgia just to see the spectacle of waves
clapping and stroking the rocks, of light playing
on fluid, ever-moving fields, of this domain
we've managed, under siege, to keep free, this
undulant-as-the-ocean's rollers land mass.
Unselfconscious pilgrims, treated here by some
with derision, disdain, they can't believe
                              that this is earth.
How can residents bend over books or knit?
When we're ferried over the threshold of Death,
and our breath is *actually* taken from us,
will we be struck with greater wonder than this?

5

CLOVER

Not by any effort of mine
or anyone else's
do the soft pale plum brushes
of this flower bend up among the grasses,
dabs of its opposite to alleviate the green,
to feed the bee and the cow
fodder for the promised honey and milk.
Not cultivated, tended, fertilized,
through vast root mats,
they are suckled by the sod
and each petal is a tiny claw
to draw down from the sky
sun and water.
That they are common, mass produced,
has not given excuse
for corner cutting, the use
of inferior materials.
Quality is assured.
Every ovate leaf is sealed, as if by hand,
with a silvery "v," chevron of modest rank:
wishbone, wingspread, moonhorns – grail.

UP WITH FISHERMEN AND BIRDS

As sun casts its first and rosiest glow
over the water and lobster boats
motor out to drop or pull their traps
swishing deftly as courtiers the long train
of their wakes around buoys bobbing colors
proud as heraldic coats over the sea's
wave-smoothened field, as captains
in orange waders stand at the helms,
or lower traps over the gunwales,
their engines rasping like morning
trying to clear its throat; as deer bow
in an attitude of worship, into the mist
hovering just above the meadow,
their backs caught tawny in the rising light;
as bees make their gold-gathering rounds
of poppies, balm and mallow; as crows
harangue each other; as the hummingbird whirrs
to probe the fuchsia for its breakfast juice
and the phoebe keeps putting its name
before the world; as the morning glory
composes itself in the shadows waiting
for a spotlight before it blows its horn zenith blue,
the poet too is awake and at it at this hour,
seated in her cerulean chair on the porch.
Binoculars handy, books stacked around her,
she bears witness to the beginning, embellishing
the fresh, clean pages of the day with words of praise
that we have once again come whole, come new
                              out of the dark, out of the dark.

CLOTHESLINE

I pin my words up: fuchsia, orange, turquoise shirts, stripes, solids,
tees or tanks, that rhyme or clash with purple pants, threads stressed
by work or bulges: skirts tarantella twirled alliterative with towels,
the nap of which has dabbed every curve I've lain on sheets
inscribed with wild love; caesura socks, confessional briefs
with shame-stained crotches; apostrophic bras prosthesis pocketed,
a tablecloth for underlying dishes which elicited from diners
voluptuary vowels; rags, suits, slips, quilts, aprons, napkins, hot
pads, throw rugs, swimtogs – everywoman's load of nouns;
plus strange, belaced lavender gowns. They flap against the sky
like pennants, like wagging tongues. My whole life's on this line.

for Eugene Vance

BLACK LOCUST

Every Spring I'm afraid you're dead.
Last week of May, first of June,
then second, every tree around you
garrulous with green, you stand silent,
branches corkscrewing into the clouds,
bare as November's end.

Way out of your range, like me,
you're a Maine-loving Midwest transplant
mad to root in the sea's view.
I count on you, comrade, big pea,
overgrown vetch, to come on thick
with frond-like panacles articulate
with lovely, thumb-shaped leaflets the wind
can tousle, can whip, but rarely remove.

You're supposed to be strong.
You're supposed to be ship's mast,
rot-proof fence posts, so why
aren't you coming through?
Many of my other neighbors are failing
or fallen. I'm not so solid myself.
I can't lose you too. It's been
consoling to think of you outlasting us
still towering, our ashes feeding your roots.

By now you'd think I know the drill:
you dawdle. You wait till it's completely
safe, not even a leaf toe in the air
until it's almost solstice. But I panic.
I've been trained to conclude that
if everything else is leafing now,
you should too, or else something's
awfully awry. I jump to the worst
to head it off, to keep from being
completely let down.

9

Just when I give up, though, you put out.
One by one, then suddenly a mass
of leafy wands like sprays taken
to hail a queen and her entourage.
You shake them at everything around you:
grasses, gulls, vehicles, wires, roofs, the sky,
dubbing it all noble. I'm so glad
my window frames as prospect – you.

SUN

for PG

She has the effect on me of sun,
of sun on seedlings beaten down
by rain, a week or more of storm.
Tenuous at best, not fully rooted,
they look as if they won't take hold,
will never again straighten
the spine of their stems, as if
their leaves will always droop.
But light and warmth evaporate
what weighs them down.
They lift and shift to know this truth
and that what battered them,
punishing as it was, was
water, nurture necessary too.
They rise up and grow out of themselves
beyond even what they dreamt,
free in sun's encouragement
to launch into the wild blue.
This is what only minutes with her does.
For she has grown so and bloomed
by submitting to the influence of a star.

EVERYDAY WONDERS:
Oases for a Grief

Will the rain never stop? Day after day
tears drip and drip and drip off the roof.

First up, first to flower, chives.
Before they can emerge, the bristly purple
blossoms have to split a translucent lavender caul.

Streamers of fog are lain along a stretch of coast
as if to cordon it off, to mark its deep green trees,
its tawny rock for special notice.

The earthworm's naked glistening length
noses its long journey across the road accordion-wise,
front rings stretch apart, then press together,
back ones a beat later, pulsating forward.

At dusk the blossoming apple is alive
with subtle movement, a flock of cedar waxwings
rummaging through the fluff, nipping bugs.
Like pale yellow flames, their breasts, licking
                              through the branches.

A floss spider, the single seed
floats on its filaments toward indeterminate ground
in which to push down its root and spread its leaves wide.

for Dorothy Silvers

NEIGHBORHOOD

I emerge from the tangled bedclothes
of love: turmoil, comfort, passion, heartbreak.
What does it all come down to?
And why do I try to figure it out,
unable to entertain at once all modes?
Pulling up the shade on a clear summer's dawn,
pink light stealing over the neighbors' roofs,

I catch him, paramour across the road,
wheeling away from her door.
He ignored her eyes, arch and startled,
and took her, it seems, so stunning,
so young, to console his loss, to extend
beyond the limits of his body. And she
hoped he would be her transport.

Two houses down, the old guy, half blind,
stumbles with his black retriever
around and around his potato field
moaning, Oh! *Oh!*
Without his mate now, disoriented,
he parts the vines with his cane
searching for some way out.

The artist down close to the shore
burned into night the yellow lozenge
of her studio window, trying,
so precise in line and color,
to get straight why her husband
turned away from her years before.

Next door in his shed out back
the professor practices on his oboe
the dance, with some missteps, across
a staff of notes, high, delirious, baroque:

a new wife, a baby daughter – the first coupling,
sons stuffed into lower registers.

The couple on the corner
cannot contain themselves.
Do they loom so large
so as never to be slighted?
Their only comfort, seemingly,
their domain's control,
patrolling their borders.

Out back the widow wakes again
from the embrace of her dead husband.
Artful with thread, with petals,
pixels, seasonings,
she cannot conjure the feel
of his skin against hers, his dry laughter.

The sea keeps reaching for the shore.
How patiently the mountains stand
under constant vicissitudes of cloud.
Weathers waft; they pound and pour.
Gathered on common ground, we're
held together in the precincts of this hour.
So close, yet so alone – we don't even know
our own whole stories, inhabitants of now
homing in the realms of yonder.

NEW MOON

After a day of hearing ugly words
fired between those once friendly,
each of whom I love;
of only grudgingly acknowledging
my own needs to guard property,
to seize control; of trying to ignore
war news, children's bullet-riddled
corpses borne from the streets
by grief-shrieking parents
in neighborhoods just like ours,
I lift my eyes to you,
slice of light, pinkened
by high summer sundown,
backed by broken bands
of charcoal blue clouds.
High, not judging, just
above, you hold up,
serene, an imago
for our torn-to-pieces world.
I wish I could slip through
the quicksilver slit
you make in the dark
into a brighter realm.
But for the moments I stand under you,
promising fragment, fresh-start crescent,
looking up, I sense from what has been
sundered a wholeness can grow,
as you do when you make the rounds
of our fractured globe visiting on all –
the curling leaf of a deep-forest fern,
the crushed, slimy Styrofoam cup –
a nimbus gentle and pale.

BUG BOY

for Ben Weibel

There is a whole world
we who are too tall
are not appreciating enough.
Ben will show it to us.
At five, when asked, he says
he wants to be an *"entomologist,"*
as he picks a grasshopper out of the air
mid hop and holds it up to admire
its cool GI Joe camouflage,
its back legs angled ski jump-wise.

I tell him when I was his age
we had a plague of them.
I was scared to go out.
They came in a big black cloud
and covered my driveway
like a squirmy tarp.
Ben breaks into big smiles.
*That would have been
a good old time for* **me**!

He catches flies by the wings
and lets them go
the way other kids might
pat a buddy on the shoulder.
Didn't we see that spider
on our stair step? He checks
to see if it's "venomous."
Too late. It's slipped
into a hole, even when
we bend down, too small to see.

He visits us after dark
just to watch moths
cavort around our porchlight,
claps one between his palms
cracks them to take a peek.
It flies out; he laughs,
I'd do that too if it was me!

He may be the only human
admirer of the earwig.
He's treasured one
in a big Ball jar
with a hole-poked lid –
he's got at least ten –
along with a beetle
big and black
as those found for
reanimating the dead
in Egyptian tombs.
He lets it crawl
over his hands like a babe
over a trustworthy parent.

He found it helping his dad
jack up the garage
and pour a new foundation.
After work they go down island
to "the snake field" to relax,
to indulge a side passion.
Like a stepson
of the ancient Cretan goddess,
he never fails to hold one aloft,
its turquoise belly wriggling.

Since he was old enough to walk,
a blue butterfly net has been
just the best of all his stuff.

Favorite pastime: looking
under rocks – hours of it.
Will those answers be the same
in his high school yearbook?

Sack race at the Fair.
Like every kid there, he wants
to be first to cross the line.
Halfway down the field a dragonfly
zooms by. Not to stop,
to take in that glittery greenness
would be to him a snub,
something precious missed.
So he does; the others
keep jumping toward the finish.
The prize? He's already got it:
pinching that luminescent body
gently between his fingers
its wings whirring.

BEE BALM

Assured and sturdy-stemmed they rise,
higher than other rain-rotted, snail-snacked plants:
jesters' scepters, jack-in-the box surprise, fiery spiders,
flush, whoosh, a gusher – red,
redredred, arms raised, hands arced fandango,
a claw to snag the sun at "high," at "up," at "hot."
Hummers' nectar bar, apian opiate,
they could be fury too long held down
busting out glad, blood, at last,
given its unruly-haired head.

CROW ISLAND

This tussocky, bed-headed knob
accessible by foot only hours a day at low tide
across a bar of rocks with barnacle acne
has barely enough level ground
for a person to stretch out on,
let along to build up. Its so rocky shore,
might as well warn: don't even *think* of mooring.
As far as anyone knows it isn't even owned.
Left to her own devices then, nature here
can part-ay, with little interference
from us, and she treats the space as a teen
would her own room: seaweed strewn
like clothes thrown off and left
for someone else to pick up. The same
with shells shattered and empty –
might as well be bottles, wrappers, cans
after a throw-down tossed. On some outcrops
the lichen could be beer-colored spills.
All sorts of grasses show up with top knots
anything from long and flowy to crew.
As for flowers, the gamut; it's a popular haunt,
a gang hang out: rose and primrose, beach pea,
toadflax, eyebright, skullcap, yarrow, thistle
and wild radish – they're especially hot –
blooming not in neatened, sectioned plots
but wherever they damn well please.
Out here it's helter skelter. It's willy nilly.
A clique of spruce, who can take – bring it! – whatever
the wind's got, squatted on the topmost spot
getting dibs on the primo view, 24/7, 360:
not-so cut, buffed round mountains, far out islands,
the mainland's harbors and docks, its clapboards,
sailboats, workboats, yachts, the cloud-flown lid,
the open drink singing blues so loud they shriek
with the no-word-could-ever-nail-it name of God.
Flight paths of gulls, ospreys, hawks are their invisible tags,
their amen crisscross over this scene, so way cool.

SLIME MOLD

for Winfried Boos

In damp woods shadowy, deep,
a glob of yellow, tansy bright,
plopped right at my feet,
luminous mucus hawked from
a gelatinous sun. It creeps
over leaves and needles, twigs, duff,
ravenous for classy bacteria.
A palate highly refined or
fiend for microrganisms?
It's a plant (fungous).
It's an animal (amoebic).
It's a natural phenomenon.
To an ant, a tidal wave of lemon curd,
to a bird, one of its eggs splatted.
Propelled by whiplash flagella
or pseudo-limbs, it morphs
into blobby, pimply plasmodium
teeing up fruited bodies
pocked as golf balls
which then elongate and erect gantries,
Canaveral-wise, to rocket off spores.
Scram! They're out of here,
stored, God knows where, incognito
in Mother Earth's witness protection program,
till good and ready – could be years –
to reemerge. It's SO random!
Could an order be contrived
more curious than this one?

CAPRELLA MUTICA

for Karin Boos

Because there is no funding
to study the merely beautiful,
she shifted her focus from her real love,
brittle stars, ancients with radial symmetry,
long, rippling arms and fantastic
survival strategies, like burying themselves
in sediment to escape predators, to these
skinny little buggers.
She reaches under the dock,
brings up a wad of algae,
and slops it with seawater into a small
Tupperware tub. Clinging to
and swimming around the gunk
are skeleton shrimp, once
native only to the Sea of Japan,
but now, because of global shipping,
they've turned up here, on the other side
of the world and become invasive species;
hence, a possible economic threat,
thus, more likelihood of funding for study.
She's spent three years of her youth with them
on an island in the North Sea one kilometer long,
and in daily – all day – contact they've
endeared themselves to her. The way one would
a valentine or a child, she calls them *her* creatures, *hers.*

An inch long and thinner than a fishing line,
in these parts, they're called alien and look like it,
look too like petraglyph stick figures, with antennae
sprouting wild from their heads to gather food
into their mouths, with their miniscule claws,
three sets of legs lower down and, at the bottom,
a tuft of rudders. She learned by watching

22

closely and long, that they have sex after molt
when, without their barely perceptible
shells, the females are more penetrable; that
the "grandmothers" form a protective kindergarten
circle around the hatchlings. Once she points it out,
we can tell the pregnant females easily
by the obvious bump of the brood sac
in their middles. They scootch around
like inch worms, sometimes in manic watusi.
Darting among them are marine wood lice, black mites
she calls "sweet," who raft across the Atlantic on seaweed.
It makes me believe we might be redeemed as a species
that there are such humans, *tumpel typs*, who, fascinated
by tiny lives beneath the notice of most, dive into a handful
of water, spend their days in awe of an on-earth universe
and establish intimate relationships with their hosts.

RUDBECKIA

for Kathy Graven, Encarnations:
Dennis, Luke and Dave

When they came to this northern, rock-rimmed isle,
they made Italia of their plot of ground,
raised-bed gardens spilling over the fencetop
a whole spectrum of petals, delectables.
Though it might take years for them to yield, they sunk
into this rocky soil fruit trees unheard of
in these latitudes: peach, cherry, pear, plum.
Their goal: to see blossoms out every window,
to make it so happy it would shout!
Some neighbors wondered what
the heck they were up to. Why,
they were *changing* the way it was!
Even the crankiest, though, had to smile
when they saw the whole side yard
light up as if it had been struck with a sunbolt.
These new owners had lost their mothers young.
There'd been a recent illness, other losses too.
With that slew of black-eyed susans,
petals like yellow blades, epees,
they meant to slash it all and cancel it
with gloriosa gold.

BEAUTY BUSH

(Kolkwitzea amabalis)

for Mr. Stevens

Once I would have wished for a dream.
I might have needed to invent a bower
and place myself under it, one
that showered me with blossoms
to drown out shouting and the rain of blows.
But such tumult for the moment has slowed,
and this bush has bloomed on its own in my yard.
I can see it now, where I couldn't before.
Trouble has blown the scales from my eyes.
It is more real, sir, I believe,
than the one I might have imagined.
What is it drove you to that other home
and why did you there abide?

I could never have devised a pink
this delicate, nor the butter yellow center
veined with orange at the entrance
to each flower, the puffs of fuzz
along the stems, beneath the sepals,
the impression the whole bush gives
of perpetual upwelling, a fountain
plush and fluffy, effulgent, of cumulus
pinked by sunup. I might go too far
to say the throats of each blossom
glow with the moment of shattering –
our hopes for gold – that they are the cries
at those times we utter, that these designs,
their segmentation, remind me of Haida
totems: eagle, frog, bear, salmon.
I would be applying my mind too much,
imposing civilization on the natural.
Hasn't enough of that been done?

To increase my capacity for reverence,
to hold what comes up, unbidden, before me,
to let it shiver in breeze off the ocean
and to fall into stillness, to feel the full force
of a blow in my tissues as it hits: this, this.
If I could allow the structure of language
to collapse and enter into pure apprehension,
impossible, though thoroughly worthy
to attempt, then my guess is I might
experience the essence of what before
I thought I would contrive, though
amplified when unfettered by my limits.
The world as given, brutal and beautiful, *amabilis*,
is too riveting for me to leave it willingly,
supreme though they seem, dear sir, for fictions.

MOSS

It thrives when tucked in the woods, in one
of the island's coverts. In dappled sun,
in the cool of soothing shade,
a mottled collage, an arresting array
of tones and textures: from sage, celadon,
citrine, bottle, emerald, olive, Irish
to verdigris, reseda accented with damask
in bumps, humps, mounds, knobs,
soft, solid, springy, spongy, starred –
fuzz, fluff, fleece, chenille, velvet, velour.
On the floor of the forest against a background
brown of needles and leaves lies a hideaway
inviting to the tired: pillows plumped,
cushions, carpets, futons, comforters.
Lay me down on them.
Lay me down beneath these trees.
And let me green.

NOTE

for PG

On the artist's back
the wind writes
in flowing folds
of her blouse
a furious cursive
of thanks
for paying attention
to these islands and hills,
this sea, this sky,
for trying
minute by minute
to approximate in paint
changes earth's turning makes
in the blues,
to convey, as if moving,
a cloud,
and, with all else
humans could choose,
for devoting a whole morning
solely to this view.

LUPINE BLOOM

At solstice,
congregations
of them gather
by the road in fields
to witness
the apogee of light.
They assemble,
they mass,
straight-spined,
upstanding, spiked,
each vertebra
distinct,
each a harmonium
of color, solids
containing with them
hints of other hues.
Purple licked
with pink and vice-versa,
white with blue:
chord progressions
ascending, scaling the sky.
Or they could be organ pipes.
They could be temple
columns made
of racemes, petals
arrayed around an axis stem,
foils to spear the year
at high. Silently,
they watch us passing,
our procession, flowers
named for the wolf,
knowing each bloom's hood
conceals a gold-dusted fang
to get into time a tooth.

Before the peak
and turn downhill,
they lift their spires.
They stand at attention,
dignified, vigorous,
expiring too.

TWO

for Bea Weinreich and Naomi McShea

If you saw them walking, one feisty
and double-timed, slightly stooped,
the other tall but slowed to a steady lope
by treatments for a dread disease;
if you noted their grays: one thin
but elegant as veils overlaying chic
1940's millenary, the other pale
and smooth as certain ocean-honed stones,
each still dark, lively-eyed beauties,
it would not be astute to assume
they were too old to produce,
from the piano, the mandolin, passages
of Beethoven, Bach, Mozart, Vivaldi
with a passion far more ardent
than that of any youth.

Though they didn't meet till middle age,
one, as a child, lived down the street
in the Bronx from the iron monger's shop
of the other's father. With so many ways
to choose the use of precious days, every
morning they show up at the church. Naomi's
hands, poised like wings of a monarch arched
over buddlea's purple torch, come down
confident on the keys. Bea plucks quarter note
tremolos as if from heartstrings
of foremothers fleeing the pogroms.

They launch grinning into music new to them,
shrugging off fumblings, egging each other on,
quipping and kidding in Yiddish.
Their counterpoint temperaments:
warm, smiling and gentle but earnest;
sharp and definite but teasing and deep-hearted
intertwine through notes rising and falling
on a staff, like morning glory vines
climbing over wires into flower.
They take to the clefs as if to native elements
taking measures on them against death,
against losses of beloved husbands,
against a world determined still to harm
whomever it labels "foreign,"
and it's like taking the waters, bathing
for resurgence in eternal tempos and modes.
Side by side, in their instrument ships
they're taking the *waves* – peaks and troughs,
it's all the same sea – and being swept,
as they couldn't be alone, out beyond themselves,
beyond the sight of home into higher octaves,
sublime harmonics – sublime.

WEIRD THINGS IN MY NEIGHBORHOOD

Start in a garden bed near the road
with the plastic frog which ribbits most times you pass it,
recently replaced by a lighthouse up-to-your-nose high
with bits of seaglass plastered in its sides
and a bulb in it bright enough to blind you to the stars.

Move on to the wall of sunflowers so thick, so tall,
planted by new over-exuberant gardeners, it blocks
their view of the water!
                          Then to the boulder barricade
installed after a drunken truck slammed into a car parked out front.
Ounce of prevention? Pounds of appallment?

                    How about the jerryrigged bike
with a hinge that allows the front wheel to cant at an angle
to the road left and right? When asked the advantage of this,
the maker only flashed a smile.

                        What would you make of a rope
wound round and round the trunk of a maple and up into its branches
put there ostensibly, when extended, to make a dog run?   For years
never cut, untangled or removed, it makes the tree look like a tied up
hostage.

            Never sure how much she wants passersby to see
of her world-class garden, a certain neighbor plants spruce seedlings
one year to half-conceal the view and the next, tears them back out.

Then there's the architect's shed built when he was 10:
rotting, ramshackle, half fallen in, light slicing through gaps
in the walls, an open hole near the roof – its only use
storage for a pea fence. How it contrasts with the prize-winning bark
whose floorboards he recently soaked and bowed, seamlessly joined
and varnished to high, fine gloss.

                                        Why would ice skates
be slung all summer over the crossbeams of the porch
of non-winterized cottage or irked, absent owners expect their
untended garden to provide them with lettuce when they return,
or smiling angels, smiling cats, smiling fish painted on heart rocks be
left around the steps of the house mostly vacant now due to divorce?

Come away refreshed from our making-sense-free zone
where little is "set right" because we're not sure what
"right" is, and be consoled , released from the need
to tie everything up neatly. Or better yet, set
your windshield-less truck out back and let it nest
in the brush for eons like great pale green hen to brood.

ISLAND
JOURNAL

Maine has persisted as a culture of small villages, a society
characterized by identity with place and strong tribal feelings
of kinship for its own and with the land.

– Lew Dietz
Night Train at Wiscasset Station

ISLAND JOURNAL

It's the Fourth of July afternoon. We have just come back from the island picnic under the maples on Ruth Westphal's front lawn where the Declaration of Independence was read among many-versioned and way-more-than-we-needed bowls of baked beans and potato salad. We're sitting on our porch with neighbors going through *The Times*, our Sunday concession to the rest of the world. Actual news out there today is thin, but portentous: speculations of how Iraq will govern itself now that power has been transferred, predictions about the upcoming elections here, all that rides on them along with assessments of past presidencies because of Reagan's death and Clinton's book coming out. I am struck with a pang of fear. How much longer will we have the luxury of lazing about like this contemplating the world's ills from afar? Will jack-booted history ever tromp up the steps of this porch to threaten and banish our way of life here?

The island mischief-makers just flew past in their old pickup that now will only go backwards. The driver and riders are accused but never arrested for various island break- ins involving mostly the plundering of stashes of alcohol. Last night many islanders were awakened by this crew's middle-of-the-night private fireworks fest. Many are worried that the driver will hit a child or someone else, but no one has confronted him out of fear that their house will be the next break-in target. On the pickup is a black garbage bag rigged to look like a sail. Behind it flaps, as they zoom by backwards, a large American flag. A kind of pirate land vehicle.

Our view has been slightly altered this year by the remodeling of a neighbor's house. They added a screened in porch and a tall stone chimney. They bought the house three years ago from artists and have fortified it to accommodate two young children. If the chimney were not so handsome and the new addition so finely built, trimmed in dark green paint, and had we not quickly grown to like the members of this boisterous, creative household, it might bother us more, as it clips a few feet of what we can see of our most cherished and familiar body of water: the Western Way.

This morning first thing a neighbor's seven-year-old son, a boy I consider my friend and also, actually, my superior, hailed me on the road. He had arrived near midnight the night before from Seattle. From the field he held proudly aloft by its tail what he announced joyously to be "the first snake of summer" and showed me how the snake was trying to strike at him. This will be only the first of his entomologic and herpetologic discoveries I'll have the honor of sharing with him in the next weeks. It was a small, non-poisonous snake, about 18 inches long with a black and yellow tweed design on its back. When it opened its mouth the color inside was pale pumpkin. It wriggled marvelously and disappeared into the tall grasses when Ben set him down.

Everyone on an island needs to help with *something*, whether she is qualified or not. I am on the building committee for the historical society. One of the native islanders is selling an old building on her property to the society for a generously low amount. It will be moved to a piece of donated property to become new, more spacious housing for the museum, which is now located in what was the old schoolhouse. (The school closed a couple of years ago due to lack of students, but babies are being born on the island, raising hopes of its opening again. Hence the need for the museum to find other housing.) The building to be moved was once a dining room where "rusticators" came to take their meals, and though it has been used for many years only as a storage house, it has been declared by inspectors as uncommonly sound. My job is to decide where the drive to this relocated building should be placed and how the property should be landscaped. My only qualification remotely relevant to this task is being a private, moderately successful gardener, but on islands you have to use whatever resources might be at hand, however meager! One of my concerns as I make some decisions is that, since the parsonage will be next door and I have lived in parsonages myself, I want the plantings and the placement of the drive to retain as much privacy as possible for the parsonage residents. I'm suggesting a diagonal, winding path with native plantings in the crooks of the drive: potentilla, lupine, grasses, rosa rugosa, and a hedge of fast-growing spruce between the museum and the parsonage.

A couple of years ago open season was declared on the island to "cull" the deer population – a controversial decision. There was a bloodbath: carcasses left by the side of the road and months when it was unsafe for year-round residents to leave their homes for fear of gunfire. One outcome of this decision, I noticed this week, is that all along the shore by the dock, there is now a foamy, serpentine bank of pale yellow wild radish blossoms. I remember finding one or two by the shore in years past and identifying it for its cruciform positioning of four veined petals. Now, amongst a host of many other wild flowers previously not growing here, the radish produces a lovely, rampant ruching along our edges with no deer to nibble away at it.

Tonight I am enjoying a quiet, contemplative night at home, the first in some time with no off island guests, no invitations out, no one coming here for dinner and no concerts or other island events to attend. It is the illusion of those who have not lived on islands that it is always quiet and solitary here. Rather, in summer, it is an intensely intimate and active community. Socializing is complex since everyone knows all the players and their bikes or vehicles and can tell who is having dinner with whom. It's a cloudy evening with long strands of fog suspended just above the water. I've craved quiet like this. But I see our neighbors drifting home from parties they have been invited to – and we not – and a streak of loneliness runs through me, of not belonging. Were we not invited because I don't drink or am dull, because my husband, though he can tell a risqué joke with the best of them, is a minister? Have I inadvertently slighted or offended someone? Or is it something completely not having to do with my egocentric imaginings? A favor returned or a special affinity I have no part in? Having been an isolated, homely child with inch thick glasses and a troubled family, I always feel left out at such times, though I may have been at a dinner party the night before enjoying the food and company but also wishing I were home reading or listening to music. How to account for the inescapable perversity of one's own nature!

It's strange that I who am so profligate and often wasteful, have small corners of thrift that exhibit themselves in yard work. Today I pruned the lichen-ridden, red-flowering honeysuckle, just as its blossoms were going. This may not be a good time to do it. I can never keep track of when it's good to prune particular bushes. Lilacs, right after flowering is all I can remember. Otherwise, it's "when I'm in the mood," and today I am. This bush is right outside our living room window and must be very old. I pruned it mercilessly last year, and behold! it did come back fuller than the year before. But it still has many small dead branches. Birds are attracted to this bush, and if I stretch out on the couch and am quiet, I often have a wonderful close look at a yellow warbler: rusty chest streaks, standing out against its brilliant yellow. Most memorably, one August, a host of cedar waxwings descended on the bush's red berries. What a feast for me too! Instead of throwing them out into the field, I've saved the dry ends I snipped off for kindling. And as it happens, my husband just needed them for the fire he was building to warm our 50 degree midday July chill.

A couple of years ago trash burning was banned on the island. We had several drought-ridden years and open trash burning became hazardous. Also, new state environmental regulations have prohibited it because of air pollution. I miss the practice of trash burning. Over the years we had a succession of metal contraptions, ending with an oil drum topped by a gerry-rigged screen. It still sits rusting out back. I continue to burn small amounts of paper waste in the wood stove, but it was so satisfying to see all that cumber (as the Quakers call it) be taken so swiftly by the flames.

Across the road our itinerant carpenter (he winters wherever the jobs are along the southern coast: Florida, the Carolinas) is taking much longer than our neighbors want him to to finish replacing their double-decker porch, which, after 50 years, was sagging with rot. A couple of years ago, he rebuilt our upper deck, part of which blew off in a straight line wind storm. I remember being similarly perturbed by his pace, but he is a fine and meticulous worker, and I appreciate his attention to detail. He spent a long time matching the lattice work he replaced on our deck to what remained, making sure all the slats in each section were slanting the same way – something I never would have noticed. The result is that no one would ever know there had been damage done. I've always marveled at the red truck he barges onto the island every year. It has sides that slide up to reveal all his tools and materials neatly sectioned and tiered, arranged by size and function. When he wants a certain brace or nail, he never has to rummage for minutes – or longer! – as I would. He knows *just* where to find what he wants and reaches for it immediately.

This year I arrived here from the Midwest two weeks later than I usually do, June 13. I had been ill most of the winter and, at the time I came on the island, had a respiratory infection and a stiff neck and shoulder, both probably somehow the result of the tiring 1700 mile solo drive. I really didn't think I'd have it in me to make a garden this year, but dreaded a summer of staring out at blank plots. Out back is a fenced 25' X 25' garden and, on two sides of the house, a 4' deep wraparound border. I also felt how late in the season it already was, though encouraged, when I heard it had been a cold, wet Spring, so a head start was not necessarily advantageous. No sooner had I informed two friends already here of my condition, but they arrived the next day with hoes and rakes and spades. I hire a local teenage boy to rototill the plot, which he had done, but my friends with my rather pitiful one-armed assistance sifted out all the grass and weeds and rocks and made the plot smooth as a blank page. The longer we worked, laughing and talking as we went, the better I felt. Then, one of them showed up the NEXT day too, to plant seeds. On an island there is still a vestige "barn raising" culture, where neighbors gather to help the one who's had impairment or misfortune. This was one deeply moving example to me. I am now enjoying with more gratitude than usual the plants sprouting and flowering.

After a trip to the Aegean, I painted our front porch Adirondack chairs Greek Island blue. Daytrippers started stopping to take pictures of our house and front garden. I try to make that garden as multi-colored and multi-textured as possible, and no doubt cram too many plants in the space – some 40 or so species of perennials and annuals in a roughly 4' X 25' area. But at the peak of the season, when everything's blooming, it is quite a riot of color, a floral fiesta. It's interesting to note the conflicting feelings of gratification for and rebellion against being others' idea of "picturesque" that rise up in me when people stop to ooh and ahh. I'm glad the garden gives pleasure to passersby, whether "on island" or "from away." That is part of the joy I get out of arranging it and tending it to blossom. But there's an objectification that takes place once a picture is snapped, as if the one who snaps it can now carry part of me away without asking permission. It gives me a "gotcha" sense of having "been framed" and creates a sad and infuriating separation between me and whoever takes the picture.

Over the last few years, I'm afraid too many of us on the island have formed an unofficial "cancer club." Dear neighbors have died of it, and some of us have survived. After the boost my friends gave me with my garden, I started to feel stronger and passed on their "mitzvah" by planting all blue and purple flowers (a wish she expressed last year) in the planters of an older friend down the road who has fought hard with a kind of leukemia: several shades of lobelia, alyssum, angelonia, forget-me-nots, heliotrope, petunias, ageratum, phacelia, brachycome, browallia, etc. She is only able to come for a couple of weeks this year when her daughter can be here to help her. We share a love of this portion of the spectrum and also the feeling of restoration and delight that having flowers nearby can give. I wanted for the short time she'll be here for her to have the blessing of their soothing, undemanding company.

On our kitchen table is an old clock radio, a hand-me-down from my sister-in-law when we bought our house 16 years ago. About 10 years ago, the digital clock stopped working, so the hour started flashing random times in blue: 6:50, 4:33, 2:15, etc. Then, some years later, after many attempts to fix it, it just kept flashing 12:00 on and off night and day. In the middle of the night, if I came down to make a cup of Sleepytime tea, it acted as a kind of bizarre, strobe nightlight. Why did we not replace it with one that worked? The radio gets great reception, and, since we have no TV here, NPR is a very important link for us to the outside world. Last week a guest, one of several over the years who have been driven wild by the clock, fiddled with the dial and got it to stop flashing. Now it reads perpetually 4:25, AM or PM, I'm not sure. Not everything CAN be fixed, so keeping something that can't and just letting it be gives me a sense of ease, a freedom from perfection and the satisfaction of driving certain guests crazy!

Last night a neighbor down the road, a year-round resident, beat and verbally abused his wife at a party, witnesses said. She was taken away and hidden at a friend's house. We didn't hear it, but the husband apparently tore up and down the island drunk in his pickup and then broke into two other houses shouting for his wife before locking himself in his own home with 20 or so guns. Now a SWAT team, first in memory ever to come out here, has set up a roadblock and surrounded the house. The husband refuses to come out. Having experienced enough violence in my own home growing up, I've stayed put and have not, as others have, wandered up the road out of curiosity. I had just seen the husband two days ago in his yard painting the too-small boat he uses for lobstering. He was going over the lettering of the boat's name in appropriately-colored paint: "Red Devil." He used to cut our lawn, cut wood for us and helped me plow up the sod for my garden. He once asked me if he could trade some lobsters for a copy of my book, one of the greatest compliments I ever received. I've always prayed he would seek help for his drinking. If they get him out of his house, he may be forced to. His wife is a talented artist and our postmaster, whose pleasant competence each of us experiences when we go to get our mail every day. In Minneapolis, where I live in the winter, if this happened a couple of blocks away, I might at most hear an anonymous siren and think nothing of it. On an island everything is intimate and intensified. It is impossible not to feel and be affected by what happens to everyone.

One evening a couple of weeks ago (I'm only able to write about it now), I was crossing the road, as I often do before dinner, to borrow a can of mandarin oranges a friend had for inclusion in our salad. Behind me after I'd crossed, our dear Jack Russell terrier, Birdie, bounded out the closed but unlatched screen door and was hit by the truck of a son and father coming up from the dock after a day of lobstering. My friend's husband, who was in his front yard working on his deck that faces the road, let out a terrible shriek. I froze and feared to turn around. Our dog was yelping and, as I ran back to pick her up she, gentle spirit that she was, in her panic, bit me. She was just over a year old and had been given to us by a friend on the island when she knew we were looking for a dog. Everyone acknowledged that Birdie was an unusual dog, a big soul, a happy soul who delighted in all who came into her world, including mailmen. Even inveterate dog dislikers melted when she approached them at a respectful distance, short tail wagging, peering up with lively dark eyes as if to learn who they were. No barking, no pawing, no begging for attention. Just greeting, just eager for meeting. My husband ran out of the house choked with sobbing and yelled at the guys in the truck to get us a boat to take her over to the vet. Other neighbors brought a towel to wrap her in and antibiotic ointment for my hand. I went into the house fumbling and shaking to call the vet and my husband ran with her down to the dock. But, by the time several of us rushed down to meet him, his cries echoed and tore through the harbor: *She's gone! She's GONE!* We trudged in shock and sorrow back up the hill, our friends and neighbors gathered around us. A young friend our daughter's age whose mother's grave we had helped to dig at her Jewish funeral some years ago asked us where we wanted Birdie's grave and with tears dripping off his nose, dug and dug until it was deep enough. We wrapped her in a blanket and laid many shafts of then-blooming lupine over her as our friends cried with us and held us. We gave thanks for her life and the joy so briefly we had through her. We didn't think we could bear the pain of this loss and wept in those next days until our heads split and our eyes swelled almost closed thinking of her jumping straight up and down two feet off the ground when we would return home; her special snufflings and the way her lip curled back over her tiny front teeth after she yawned; her all white face, black bespotted belly, scruffy "rough" coat and the way she rested her chin in our laps when we sat on the couch. On and on…. That same young man made chicken soup; our younger friend the entomologist brought peanut butter cookies and a handwritten note with a drawing of a centipede on it saying he was sorry Birdie had been "kiled;" a down-island friend brought, along with some cajoling humor, a warm, fragrant, hand-baked focaccia. There was a book about white dogs in heaven, and many kind words, hugs, and understanding faces. Later that night, no longer able to endure the walls of our house of grief, we went out walking in the light rain. When we returned, another friend, a practicing Buddhist, was sitting cross-legged in the misty almost-dark on the well cover near the grave. She said she was sending Birdie love, attending to her as she made her passage to the next world. It was as if many members of the community pitched in to mop up, absorb, as if at a flood, enough of our tears so we wouldn't drown in them. The guys in the truck never acknowledged to us what had happened or apologized. We wrote them a note, though, to let them know we did not, as some on the island did, hold them responsible. That truck with the father driving drunk had crashed before into barns and parked cars. But this time the sober son was driving. It was an accident. The door should have been latched, though Birdie had never broken out of it like that before. Running after me, heedless, she leapt into their path. They could never have stopped in time to spare her.

45

Last year, an artist a generation older than I who lived across from us reluctantly had to sell her house here because a bum leg made it hard for her to get around, to do the chores, get on and off the ferry, etc. I miss Edna for many reasons, but one night this week, I felt her absence especially keenly. The sun had set and the clouds moved out above us over the ocean in puffy ranks underlit by the most exquisite pink against a turquoise sky. A couple of times when Edna was here, she called me to quick come to her place closer to the shore that afforded, because it is treeless, a wider unobstructed view, so we could watch the sunset cloud formations move over us across the sky. We'd stand on her deck or doorstep together smiling silently just taking in the beauty of what was passing, of passing itself, agog at the continuously changing forms of the clouds. With how many others can we be silent and feel so connected as well? To be companioned by her high state of alertness, her fearless consciousness in this and much else – incomparable experiences that indelibly deepened my life.

In my city life I bake infrequently, usually only when several people are coming for dinner. But on the island baking is a way of life, a form of communication, an expression of love and esteem, a social currency. I bake something almost every day and so do many others. Yes, it's true we may have more time than we do in our busy city lives, though many of us do work from here, and our chores, without cars to transport things and other technological assistance, take more of our time. The giving and receiving, the pleasure of making and the appreciation of eating baked goods help bind our community together. For the friend who gave us our beloved Birdie, I will make blueberry pies for the rest of my life in thanks. There is little else she needs or wants, but she has a weakness for pie – and gingerbread, so I give her a call and tell her to come down island in her truck to pick up a "delivery." Sometimes I will walk it down the mile or so myself. A wonderful neighbor who no longer comes because she feels her age now presents too many challenges to the way of life here, used to leave "anonymous" golden, perfectly risen loaves of delicious multigrain bread on our kitchen table. She gave me the recipe (a work in itself : "mix till the beaters can only dance on top of the dough") and I watched her do it a couple of times, but I would never be able to reproduce the heavenly flavor and texture of the bread she spent years of bi-weekly bakings to perfect. My taste memory will have to serve and it serves mighty well. As a way of sharing and perpetuating his heritage, once a summer my husband stirs up a big batch of *choereg*, yeasty little braided sweet breads sprinkled with sesame seeds he learned from his Armenian grandmother. He then distributes them to waiting neighbors who *wondered* just when they'd be getting their *choereg* this summer. When a houseful of guests arrives from away, you might find a plate of someone's signature molasses cookies on your porch. There are chocolate cakes when a loved one dies or is sick (what suffering cannot be at least *slightly* alleviated by chocolate?); favorite birthday cakes we make for each other: coconut, lemon, Boston cream, spice; loaves of banana bread and packed-for-travel "monster" cookies for end-of summer farewell, or a "just because" hunk of rhubarb crisp or blueberry buckle. And various recipes for brownies fly back and forth as commonly and frequently as emails now do. Our bakerly art is a way to say, "For these few days and weeks, I'm so glad to live near you."

Across the street today three boys who are on the verge of becoming men are at it again: their summer whiffleball ritual. One pitches, one fields and one hits: *thwock, thwick.* A tipped up garden cart acts as a backstop, a bicycle angled on either side of it to keep unhit balls from going into the street. They keep at it literally *for hours!* Through my screens I can hear the hoots and haws of them razzing and cheering each other. They're testing their competence, seeing how far they can go. Right now they are bonded in egging each other to pitch into the strike-it-rich zone, to knock one into the stars. Another neighbor gets irked by their noise, tells them to pipe down, but I like the descant of hope, energy and just plain fun their game lends to whatever I'm about in my house or yard. Boys and baseball: eternal summer. Each time they hit the ball, they keep the sun high in the sky that much longer.

II

This is the place where hills loom far...
Where fields lie sunny and roads twist brown...
This is the place where orchard boughs
Are seaward turned...
And the windows shine like eyes.

– Rachel Field

OUR LADY OF NEVER MIND

for Robin Richman and Clay Taylor

Her face looks like the shell of a crab,
that orange, that hard,
but she's beaming.
A rippling purple aura springs
from her skull.
Her skin is about as smooth
as tree bark, her shape – lumpy,
but, oh well, never mind.
With her mismatched arms –
one a claw, the other a broken shingle,
she's conducting the flow of the day:
let it go as it will.
It delights her mostly – even
the pitfalls and sob stories,
especially those. Where,
otherwise, would be the interest?
Of course she's standing,
or should I say, poised,
since she has no feet, but isn't everybody?
on shaky ground. There have been
a lot of quakes around here lately.
So she's surrounded by shattered crockery,
all the substance she had really,
precious pieces she once displayed on shelves.
But – oh well, she picks them up
and rearranges them, put together
with translucent glue, into a new self,
and sprouts green glass wings
that look suspiciously like leaves.
She'll never fly, but never mind –
up through her deteriorating frame
shoot rockets and rockets of love.

51

ROCK

for Chris White

Who knew until
the University of Maine geology professor
came to our island that
this backshore is the most prominent
volcanic outcrop on the Eastern seaboard?
We could have guessed, had we been
more observant, from the sharp, black
basalt cliffs down from the Cranberry Club,
but those huge pink granite tumblers?
They look so innocent of fire.
We pick up and save the eggs they drop
to anchor ourselves. They have withstood,
after all, the ocean's constant onslaught.
And we thought what we were standing on
was solid! Where we walk and make our homes
once rushed hot and dark as desire.
You can see ripplings of that writ upon it
still, as it cooled. We had no idea
we were perched on an ancient ash heap
or what eruptions it takes to build ground.

ROCKWEED

for Bill Patterson

Most would overlook what he focuses on
with such intent or would dismiss it
as "wrack," if they even knew the term,
for what could be deemed oceanic trash.
Not the picturesque sweep of shore,
the glittering sea, nor the gold-centered rose,
he aims his lens down and close
                        down and close.
Many times his shutter clicks over
the sensuous stretch of blunt-branched
translucent bronze bobbled to float
when the tide comes up: its arch
and flow; its curl and turn.
Sprawled over rock as if it were
a luxurious sun-warmed lounge
the plant is body beloved, odalisque on a couch
complete with her treasury of shells:
purple-edged mussels of innermost pearl –
or is it the swirl of a dark galaxy
spangled with barnacle stars?
It takes an eye like his to show
with what attention to detail everything
                        is fashioned – fine striations on
the periwinkle's bulge, ridged pink
either-end tips of the whelk, their sulcate spirals,
and how subtle the slightest ruffle of a frond.

PUMP ELEGY

for Charlie Wheeler, our plumber

It's gone now, the pause, the click,
then that familiar, comforting hum,
following the turning on of faucets,
the heart of the house
keeping the flow going.
The sound of bringing up
from 100 feet underground
the water to wash hands, bodies,
radishes, dishes; the water
to boil for tea, for soups and stews
or to flush our wastes safely
away from us. It would go for hours
after a long sprinkling of the garden
with a bit of grind in a dry spell,
and we'd hear just what it took
to bloom our flowers.
Without it we're that much farther
from the Source, the teeming
rock-bound aquifers, and what it takes
after boring a well deep down
to bring us what we're mostly made of
and can live only briefly without.
We've gone from shallowell, working
above ground in the basement, to,
down in the well itself, submersible,
one of the last, even out here on the island,
to do so because the jet was worn,
so it wouldn't shut off.
Now the water comes
followed by a silence –
what it costs us clever humans
to pretend we might have made it ourselves
and not, once upon a time, carried it

in vessels of metal or clay
from rivers and springs, so heavy
we knew its absolute value.
Why do we want to keep our distance
from the elements and forget
how the waters supported us
until we broke them
to enter this world?

THE PEONIES

I have wanted to live
as they do, when, in July,
after being tucked up tight,
they fling themselves
gangbusters wide, all
their many petals
peeled to expose centermost gold,
the under ones dropping down
to receive the breeze
letting it make them tremble;
to be borne up by v's of green,
leaves cheering them full open,
day torches blood-dark
burning with time;
to, momentarily at least,
brighten the faces of passersby
who might be shouldering
unimaginable cumber,
to strike distress with magenta fire.

BENEFIT

for Renna and Lyn

When fellow lobstermen, suspending
squabbles and rivalries, gathered
from all down the coast this hard-raining day
for two of their own who require regular,
long uninsured stints in the hospital
to unclog lungs that will, however, only clear
temporarily; when these friends pushed through
the crowd that turned out in the Ladies Aid
bearing tubs, just drained, off the open fires
outside under a tarp and poured
cataracts of soft-shelled orange
onto platters waiting on a table already
laden with salads, breads, casseroles,
soups and homemade sweets that said:
We're sorry you've had to suffer,
and for this wicked burden of bills, I felt,
just for a moment, death, our stupid,
uncaring system, the clouds would have to
move aside for the love coming through.

OSPREY CRIES

This is a big predatory bird,
a raptor, *one who seizes.*
Her beak is hooked like a hawk's.
She will dive from heights,
then hover and flap
before plunging, talons first –
they're awesome, gruesome –
to grab a salmon right out of the Atlantic.
Her wingspan's wide as humans
can be tall. Then why,
as we, exploring the point,
approach on foot, slowly,
respectfully over duff
and spongy moss humps
the towering, death-silvered tree
she's assembled her nest in the top of,
branches big around as
a strong guy's biceps,
does she circle above us
letting out small, high-pitched, child-sized
cries, short bursts, as if wounded,
plaintive, entreating?
Please, leave us be, me and my family!
Our numbers are just recovering
from your toxins. No, I beg you,
not even just to point and marvel.

RESURGENCE

Hanging sheets out to dry
I thought I saw a paper scrap
blown into the field behind my house.
I went over to pick it up and found
it was a pale pink rose petal.
I looked around and deep
in the waist-high grass,
out of view from the yard or road
were rose bushes erupting
all over.

Fifty years ago, this island was banked
with over-your-head rosa rugosa.
Hedges of it put out heaps
of sour-red, vitamin-rich hips.
But then, deer swam over,
multiplying into a controversy.
They nibbled roses and other
dear-to-the-human plants
almost out of existence
setting gardeners against animal lovers,
hunters against environmentalists.

The solution was slaughter – open season,
shooting from cars, carcasses left
by roads, in woods, to rot.
Like soldiers crouching in a field,
are the roses, blood fertilized,
mustering, on behalf of the fallen,
to mount an ambrosial protest or
waiting for
the all clear?

RUTH ON HER PORCH

After work or early, before tending our small,
but, because of her fine attention to it,
highly patronized library, in her ladderback chair
she takes up her post beside a table
on which she's placed a few choice shells and rocks.
Set back from the road a bit, and above it,
shaded by old maples, it's morning gloried,
gushing petunias, the steps up flanked
by greeting brown and cream crocks
of salmon pink geraniums.
Surveying the occasional traffic, she flashes
to passersby the white of her hair, her smile,
in her lap a pile of bright fabric shards.

Mother of six, for most of her life, a nurse,
she took up quilting when her husband lit out,
a way to piece herself back together,
something to do with the fury.
She'd blot out the hurt with color,
one blessed hot pad after another,
hundreds a year, the sales of them
stretching her income to just beyond meager.
Sensitive to island dynamics, disputes, news
of war, corruptions of power, she fits and stitches
what's been cut and torn into a bordered whole:
chevron, cruciform, crazy; prints and solids
of cotton – polished, poplin, gingham, calico –
blazons of a kind and vibrant order
she would restore to the world.

COMMUNITY

When the copter from Eastern Maine Medical
circled the Ladies Aid Field
to take Herb off the island,
Lorraine had just gotten off the radio to them,
It doesn't look good. 10/4.
Red-faced and sweating, she labored,
gentle-voiced inside the ambulance
to make him comfortable.
Georgie was in there holding his hand,
whispering that it was all right to go
that Nancy Jean, their daughter, years gone now,
was coming to take him across.
Barbara Ann, another daughter, red-eyed
and teary, rubbed his temples.
Don climbed in, ducking, six foot plus,
to offer a prayer, Gracious God...
Norman stood at the rear door, stocky, stalwart.

I was headed over to their place on foot,
a casserole in my boat bag
when I met the ambulance coming toward me.
Lynn and Emmy, following behind,
motioned for me to jump in their truck.
Just this morning he'd been alert and jovial,
but the cancer had spread too far,
the pain was too sharp and he was gasping.

Gaile, a visor haloing her bushy gray curls,
stood by with the aid of her ski pole cane.
Junior Bracy in a florescent red vest
motioned the copter down. A small crowd
of witnesses, murmuring and hugging each other
surrounded Herb in respectfully-spaced rungs:
folks he'd given ride after ride to in his boat
or truck, folks whose houses he'd replumbed,

whose sheds, ramshackle from rot, he'd built back,
a grateful smile, for him, payment enough –
even some he'd shouted off his turf
if they were noisemakers or litterbugs.

Herb could be tight-lipped and gruff,
more inclined to show how he felt
by unchugging your rusty water heater
by tinkering your dead engine back to purring
than with words, and, though happiest,
probably, when taking his one engine Cessna
up and farther Down East over this rugged coast
still unspoiled, almost, long-fingered and
trying to keep hold of the sea, he was damned
if, after barging back in his vehicle
from the hospital, he'd spend his last moments
alone in that contraption. So, just as
the copter touched down – one puff, *one puff…*
Children inching forward to ask what was wrong,
shrank back when told we thought Mr. Ware
had just passed on. Kelly tore off to get Dr. Liebow,
but there was no need to confirm it.
We all knew. Herb had died as he wanted to,
out on the island among us
and the love here, the love.

                              in loving memory of Herb Ware,
                              for Georgie and their girls

FRAMBOISE

Nothing sweeter
than a raspberry, wild,
ripe, warmed by the sun,
as yet unplucked;
than firsting the birds,
to finger its fuzz,
tongue its drupelets
and feel into with your tip
the little pit
where you detached it from its cap
before you squish it –
exquisite mash –
against the vault of your mouth.
Well worth
the wade through thorns,
the stains, scratches, the rips,
just to taste this bright red moment,
its juice dripping off your chin,
the tang through your buds
forking out.

WATERMELON

There being not much of later
to enjoy it in, he suggested to me,
down-island neighbor, we cut it open
right now, the "personal-sized" melon
I brought since he told me
I might as well take back home
the rhubarb pie I made for him in the hospital
because he preferred his fruit plain.
He could be plain in his speaking too!
Was it just the emotion of the moment
or was this the sweetest, juiciest, most rubiate
fruit a tooth ever sank into, bright
in the mouth as the July day outside
his shut in, TV-in-the-background house
next to which sat his big red truck
with his late wife's name, same as his boat's,
emblazoned on the hood? Next to that
rose a yellow, cross-hatched
squared off mountain of idle,
due to his illness, traps. He was a strapping,
loose-jointed man, a hunter, a kidder, skipper
of any room he sauntered through.
When I got up to leave, he couldn't rise,
oxygen tubes pinched into his nostrils.
He took my hand – a surprise – looked
into my eyes and couldn't find the bottom.

In memory of Lyn Colby

DEAD LOW

for J

Everything is drained, exposed
bereft of watery comfort:
seaweed, mud, rubbish,
discolored dock pilings,
mooring chains, shattered buoys,
rusted launching rails, grounded
hulls, below the water line, darker.
The ramp to the float is angled
so, going up it with luggage,
an ankle could double under.
You could stumble, crack a jaw
or, going down it, lose your footing
altogether. Some rocks are briney brown
and razor sharp with barnacles.
Shore birds peck into bubbling holes
for every last juicy morsel.

But lo, a starfish stranded purple
on the cobbles among shards
of glistening shells and jewel-like
glass fragments, driftwood angels.
At this point you can see what lies under.
Even from neap the tide creeps back up
like a slivered moon to its fullness,
a mother pulling covers kicked off
in nightmare back over a shivering child.
The universe is cycled so
all that has been emptied, lost,
is, within a fathomless dimension,
found and brimming over.

JAWLINE, STRONG

Without a tooth, cheeks stubbled
and so skinny, he could slip right through
the funnel of one his traps into its "parlour,"
he lives, despite an ulcer, on coffee,
big Styrofoam cups of it, and cigarettes.
When the booze he's now sworn off
broke his marriage smack in half,
he holed up in the ramshackle house
that won't sell with twenty-one guns.
Arraignment, parole. That was some years ago.
The place is still barricaded with hulks
of rusting trucks, but there's less junk than before.
Trying to make a go lobstering from a speedboat,
debt on its engine heavy as mooring stone:
seventeen hour days hauling and checking pots,
many of which could be swept mangled to shore
or lost in the next storm, the bug market down –
he's just one blown hydraulic hose away
from losing his hold. His buoys are red
with fluorescent orange tops. Passing him,
still at it at dusk grappling with tangled line,
adjusting toggles, the water scarlet with sundown,
I wave from a friend's pleasure boat.
He waves back. Brother, I salute you.

BOG ORCHIDS

Rare now, but, used to be,
Ladies Aid members gathered rafts
to decorate the church.
It takes a depth of blackness
to produce so many calopogons
and a year of storms,
a year of punishing water.
How deep is a bog?
One wrong step and you're
into it up to your hips.
Muck and yucky stuff
you don't want to deal with!
It can suck at a tree's roots
and leave it skeletal. It harbors
the pitcher plant, vacuum nozzle,
trap, but it can give rise, too,
to these delicacies, top of the line –
the floral equivalent of truffles.
You can't have them without
this bottomless mass of sodden,
acid, low-nutriated mud:
fluttery, fringed, exotic – usually
tropical – flashes all over the sphagnum
of deep to light magenta, crested,
gold-kissed lips, petals translucent.
Casting your eyes over a hoard of them,
stemmed butterflies, streaked leapers,
you can feel rich – worth it,
all you struggled up through.

FRENCHBORO

Maybe on an outer island they don't care
as much how things look. Almost nothing
but lobster boats in this narrow harbor
their two-ways blaring into air otherwise pristine.
Very few pleasure craft.
Right by the dock, a wooden hull
collapsed, and is flattening,
boards slowly falling away from each other
like a body flummoxed by exhaustion.
The shed next to it, barely
holding together, windows
punched out, slumps.
Both just left, not cleaned up, built back,
hidden, cleared away or taken apart
and used for kindling.
Weather has made every effort to polish them.
Still, they're duller than tarnished silver.
They've given out, no good anymore
for the purpose they were intended.
No one here pretends they are
or even gives a hoot.
Why do I find them beautiful?

IN PRAISE OF FOG

Some scorn it, but I welcome
days on end – though, let us say, not
without end – of fog.
It's as if the shades are drawn
and the whole island
becomes private, intimate
a boudoir, study, sanctum.
There is less traffic.
Shh. Do not disturb.
There is thought going on.
Like a seed surrounded by warmth
and wetness, in this atmosphere
something stubborn and hard
could split open.
We can steep in it, brew:
flavors blend; the stew thickens.
This opacity, diffuse, is a shield,
protection, temporarily,
from a wider view's
demanding light, outlines,
the blare of blues.
It makes billowy
mountains of its own.
We can hone in on
the reflection in water
of a red hull
sliced by a slight wind
cubistwise into slivers
that in calm again
reassemble, and,
when the fog withdraws,
revealing point by point,
once more, each formerly
overlooked spruce,
we can receive
the world primordial.

NAMES OF BOATS

What this harbor harbors!
Rocking in rows
chomping at moorings,
vessels, various,
hauling in holds
payloads of dreams.

Quo Vadis? Escape Hatch Sojourn Quest
Skamper Meander Night Train Whim
Wayfarer Peregrination Gypsy Hot Foot
Leap Frog Rover Rambler Galavant

Cristelle Estrellia Calliope Calypso Cybele
Contessa Cressida Ariadne Imperia Chouette
Muse Miranda Amazon Ariel Pandora
Proud Mary Painted Lady Mona Lisa Nymph

Phantom Toddler Tom Cat Cygnet Bandit
Desperado El Nino Alonzo Firebrand Rapscallion
Troubadour Truant Endymion Red Baron
Schmendrick Schnooks Shipmunk Schleps
Mon Ami Donald Duck Dagwood True Blue

Ruse Impulse Impetuous Audacious
Shake Down Bander Snatch White Flash Dash
Rim Shot Mischief Sans Souci Jou Jou
Jalapeno Horsefeathers Pomp Pomplemouse
Donnybrook On a Bet Turmoil Rampage Hullabaloo

Gamine High Stakes Three Wishes Instead
Fast Forward Somersault Whiplash Javelin Medallion
Abba Dabba Sea Quel Sea Quester Beats Workin'
Good Enough Way to Go Better Yet Far Out Fubar
Ke Garne (in Nepali, What's Next?) Time Well Spent

Shannon   Emily M   Ashley Lucy   Sonja Russell
Double Trouble   Just a Pluggin'   Ho Hum   Wee Won
Plain Jane   Wages   Maine Stay   Bottom Dollar
Lion Heart   Provider   Crustacean   Bracero

Fine Point   Time   Integrity   Intensity   Premise
Good Idea   Freedom   Decision   Trust
Confrontation   Takeover   Paradigm Shift
Second Edition   Perseverance   Legacy   Endurance
Destiny   Dividend   Tartan   Watermark

Fancy   Pageant   Rhapsody Ragtime Romance
Dalliance   Glory   Euphoria   Love Story   Encore
Esprit   Paraclete   *Ruach* Aspara   Champagne
Daystar   Star Spangled   Eventide   Meteor
Whisperer   Respite   Sand Castle   Moon Dance
Bijou   Silver Spoons   Belle Epoque   Freude

Hushai   Australix   Mirage   Oasis   Boethius   Cinchona
Jericho   Jubilee   Gilead   Tantra   Karma
Caraway   Bay Leaf   *Lied*   Aria   Valhalla   Zenith
Empyrean   Kachina   Idyll   Nirvana   Shangri La

CAPTAIN DAN

Sure at the helm of his able whaler
he invites us into its pool blue interior
to zoom out of frames, our usual views,
to see what we thought we knew, anew
from other angles, from the waters.

He's learned them: how to circumvent
hidden, hull-ripping ledges; how to dodge
lobster pots bobbing out of the ocean's field
like parti-colored plants; how to work
the tides for landings and departures; how to
take wakes and through the rips, cut clean.

Way before we would, he spots
porpoises, a seaweed mat –
really a guillemot flotilla – distinctive
white wing patches against their black
massed and gleaming. Farther out now,
we're wonderstruck at wave after wave
of Acadia's mountains breaking high,
as if for the first time, over the horizon.

We get caught in the crest of his zest
for exploration, let it take us beyond,
beyond ourselves to the outer islands,
each of them plumped with a tumble of
rocky pink pillows. On one, the cliffs
are squirming. The stones turn out to be
barnacled seals. Their curious periscopes
approach us. On another, we moor
and leap ashore. If the anchor isn't secure,
dug in sand behind boulders,
"When we return," he quips, grinning,
"will not be our question."

How many wonderments! Caches
of gooseberries, chanterelles; a short
rusty traintrack extending from a quarry
to the shore; a wildfire of black-eyed Susans
blazing against padlocked clapboards;
in deep woods, low, tropical huts of moss
and fungus, made for vacationing spirits;
an abandoned intact homestead still stocked
with books and firewood, flour in the canister,
a pen laid on a dusty sheet dated ten years prior,
and the quiet, the quiet of no machines,
no humming wires, only gulls and wind
whispering in its mystic vernacular.

When we hop aboard for the return, one long
dove-blue cloud stretches above us, above
the waves braiding and braiding – a blessing hand
at *motzi* over the challah. As we draw close,
we locate our common neighborhood
our huddled homes, the whites, the grays
of their peaks and beams noble and vulnerable.

In his vessel, under cerulean, small and swift,
propelled by his ever-marveling smile,
our perspective shifts; something moves.
There's more room now: in with our breath
come drafts of the vast, this fastness.
Throttling down into the harbor, ride almost
over, he swings his craft around, bumpers
flipped out, bow line gripped, docking smooth
as the slipper's fit over Cinderella's toes.

for Dan Rome
with love and gratitude

CHANTERELLES

Fisticuffs upthrusting
from rot – fallen spruce trunks,
sphagnum moss –
what'll punch you
if you pluck a clutch
of these golden ruffles
sought after as Jason's pelt
from secret caches
closely guarded by those
who've skulked
with paper sacks
for a generation
through these woods
and, when asked
where they were headed,
shrugged, mumbled,
Just for a walk…

The outing of the whereabouts
of these plump, crenellated
clumps of buttery shroom
even to favorite family,
best buds – grounds for divorce.
Yet they are, after all, only fungi!
With a name, however, sounding
like evensong bells.
You serve them to prove
you've laid hold of
the quintessence of nonpareil,
delicious, slippery
as the instant it takes to chew
the notes, gold-toned, of them
ringing *magnificat*
through the sanctuary of your mouth.

WHITE ELEPHANT

What some jettison, others, unaccountably, want:
stiff-from-too-many-washings bath towels, a hand mixer
with one beater gone. Things you never thought
to want before you saw them: a goofy oversized,
parrot-shaped pitcher, a small amphora-like pink glass vase,
an even-though-it-has-a-slight-chip-in-it (which
you discover after buying it) turquoise plate. Old-fashioned
contraptions: a screw-top hand-crank nut grinder
with a jar to catch the grindings underneath. Why?
Because they have a certain kind of *charm.*
They give delight. And for such a price! My cupboards
are full of these bargains, these *finds.* They meet
some kind of inchoate need to replace pieces lost, pieces
longed for: green depression glass bowls; tumblers, skinny tall
to wide-mouthed squat – rippled, ribbed, etched, streaked.
Closets too: the 15 years-good-now hiking boots,
the shocking pink – where else could I find that color –
jacket. I wear them all the time. A dollar each.
Then there are the slightly stained, hand-tatted doilies,
the ceramic garlic pots dear because made by islanders long gone.

What are *these*? We Ladies Aid Fair workers all crowd around:
In a baggie from a rummage box brought in are eight 4-inch long
flat-ended green glass sticks. *Oh, I know!* one of us exclaims,
*They're "muddlers." My parents used them in Old Fashioneds
to mash the fruit to get the flavor of it into the drink.* What is this?
A three-pronged stainless steel murder weaponish thing? That's
for poking into potatoes for a faster bake. And what are they *worth*?
Over pricing we debate and debate. Too high or too low,
it won't sell. And we want them *gone*! But no one knows
what the use is for a blue aluminum cup too big for an egg
with a lip curling up around the bottom. Toothpicks?
Lip's too narrow to set the used ones on. Dip? The cup's too deep.
We give up and put it on the "Dish and Dat" table.

Why does the wooden notepad holder, the word "Notepad"
embossed on it and half scratched off, with two
dumb bunny beavers carved in the top get snapped up
and the perfectly decent, still-in-its-wrapper bathmat,
price still on not sell three years running for a fraction
of the original cost? Why, if someone dumps a box
of "fern pins" on us, does a thrilled-to-pieces buyer for them
immediately show up? We should have charged more for them
than half a buck. Two neighbors can have a falling out
reaching for the same "authentic" African mask. And you
can be haunted for years by the small, white-painted caned
rocker that nothing seemed wrong with, that seemed priced
too high for the Fair, but a lot lower than it would be
in an antique shop. You waited too long to decide. And it was gone.

When you see that magenta print dress you loved
walk down the island on someone else, when you come upon
some particularly gratifying bibelot from a place unknown
and imbued with the spirit of its former owner, and,
for next to nothing it can be yours, it's not just the things
that are given other lives. You feel like you've been given
a *billet doux* from the universe, as if something big, beautiful,
rare, strange and even sacred as a luminous pachyderm
has passed through your etheric body, a shot of luck that,
for the moment, inoculates against death.

GRASSES

If one can say that any one form of
visible plant life possesses the earth,
that plant is grass.

– Hal Borland, *Book of Days*

How could I ignore them for gaudier flora
like scene-stealing peonies, lilies,
upstaging geraniums and that
prima donna the rose, mugging,
throwing their color around?
Such conspicuous efflorescing!
But the grasses – they're everywhere.
In the background like servants, sentinels.
Without them, no soil
for glamourpusses to pose in!
They keep the earth under us from crumbling,
covering more of its surface than anything else,
keep our flesh from fading off its face
by feeding us, feeding the beasts we eat
by weaving into baskets, mats, floors, roofs.

Glamour begone!
Let's celebrate what's common.
Let's bring them to the front:
subtle, delicate, elegant – strong,
and too long passed over.
How did I finally come to notice?
Got stopped. Too sore to move,
I was forced to focus under my nose.
Stock still, I saw what had once been
all of a piece, a field, was now suddenly various.
Many species in just one swath:

Rosy clouds of switchgrass, redtop,
hovering like colored fog: quack grass,

sweet vernal always standing watch –
faithful retainers, staunch; sturdy bristled
cocksfoot; red fescue arabesques; tittering
ticklegrass; hairgrass finely arced;
foxtail and timothy, their rods, their staffs.
Spikelets at attention, leaves order spears,
hand salute; brome handkerchiefs
waving hello/adieu.

Who else vegetal would be humble enough
to act as a prop, holding up dew
for dawnlight to bejewel turning
the waking world into a vast casket
of glass beads, moonstones, opals?
And few are as hospitable to vermin: bugs, slugs,
snakes, voles, moles, or as generous,
offering themselves to nestbuilders as raw material.

Hyperresponsive to wind,
nodding, rocking at the slightest puff,
rolling, reeling in gusts, bowing low in blows,
they gyrate, undulate, orgasmic, at combing strokes,
whip every-which-way in gales.
Breezes choose their stems as tongues
to speak in secret idioms and
sweep over the earth a soft, beatifying hum.

INSECT ENVY

I envy bees and butterflies, ants and wasps
who buzz and fuss around my garden blooms.
They are small enough and otherwise
equipped with infinitesimal probes
to delve into the essence of flowers.
They gorge on it and store it. By sheer
insistence, they gain entrance to sacred chambers,
to chancels, of the blossom – those smooth pastel walls!
and plunge into pollen, into yellow,
the deep yolk-yellow of the center, the stuff
that makes life and keeps it going on.
They wallow in resplendence
and make a living of it – for however long.
That is what I want.

PINK WATER

For it, we make our way pilgrim-like at sundown –
or are we, as some say here just "going to the movies?" –
in clunkers, on rusty ten-speeds, on foot
to the end of the island or the dock
where we might catch the sky –
clouds trying to make time with the sun,
coming on strong enough
to bring up a blush on the waves.
We come worried over jobless children,
at odds hopelessly with bosses, spouses,
ashamed of hatreds, excess, faithlessness,
fearful of the test results hoping this color
will, at least for the moment, bliss over
tribulation, even if such a flush,
such a rush as if of roses to the cheeks, is only
like the whole brief, fevered course of a life,
a power surge before the lights are doused.

VANITAS

Arrange your stuff around the skull:
the honeymoon shells and pebbles,
the heirloom brooch of rubies and pearls,
the peach you dared to take a bite of,
the book into which you could delve and delve,
the shattered grail, the bottle, the bulb
whose sprout you're forcing, your huddle
of cones and cubes – little city of achievements
and dreams, your travel alarm
with the second hand jerking infernally
toward your last one, and the ticket
to the where of absolute being.
On the table your grandfather knocked together
from scrap wood, draped with a throw
woven in bright, irregular stripes by women
on the other side of the world,
set it all out, move the pieces around, notice
the shadows they cast on each other, the source
of light: from whence and how to account for it.
Does darkening affect a change of essence?
Does the death's head stand out? Is it
the organizing principle? Can you even *see*
anything else or does it fade into the objects
surrounding it? How do they stand up against
the hollowed-out eye sockets, the yellowed
fissuring bone? Does that chipped-toothed grin
leer and mock or is it a nod of indulgence,
of understanding, solidarity, compassion?
Lay all this out. This is your altar now.
And after you've painted it, made art of it
for those who come after you to see
how peerless, how ridiculous
is one life's offering to time,
then lain your brush too among the artifacts,
present it for examination by demons,
the goddesses and gods.

for EWA

THREE LOBSTERS

Three lobsters try with their claws
to hold the heavens together with the earth.
They're out of their element – the sea,
and, red as sunset, they're cooked.
Behind them are the hills trying to lend support,
but it's going badly. The brown and the blue
seem determined not to budge, not
to come one bit closer
let alone commingle.
What a crazy, futile effort!
They're snapping passionately,
grasping each the one side and the other,
though they're certain to get pulled apart.
Who will eat the feast of this sacrifice?

TRACTOR

in memory of Edgar Bunker,
for Polly Bunker and Charlene Allen

He left it on shore
pointing out toward the waves
for his return if
he came back from Korea alive.
When he didn't,
and his broken-hearted father
died rather than face
lowering his only son
into this ground that keeps
coughing up rocks –
and the funeral had to be a double one –
the islanders refused to move it,
let it stand right where he left it
as his memorial.

With rollers like a military tank's
it was meant to haul boats
into and out of water and storage.
It was meant to build a business,
a family, a life.
Generations of kids
have climbed into its seat,
taken the wheel and imagined
crushing with it enemies of their own,
to win battles for grades or love or pride.

Fifty some years on, still
not removed or destroyed,
its story's told to youngsters and the curious.
Half sunk in sand and rocks,
weathered, skeletal, it's tilted forward
and consumed by a rust
fiery and furious against
favorite sons *ever* having to go off to war.

ISLAND
JOURNAL

Is the sense of place about to become another American
nostalgia ... undone by the global economy, satellite TV, and
the virtual places of the Internet? And if so, what fate for the
sense of self and identity that place provides? ... Coming to
know over time our location's weather and slant of light, its
geography and seasons, the behavior and speech and character
of its people, we gradually understand our place as metaphor,
seeing it not only in terms of our own lives but life in general
wherever it is lived.

– Wesley McNair
Mapping the Heart

ISLAND JOURNAL

Fire

I went down to the shore one morning and heard from our selectman, who stations himself on the porch of the store every morning, that there was a fire raging in the town across the water. A swath of fog prevented us from seeing the smoke, but earlier, others reported seeing it rise and then, higher, send a plume off to the east. Some had been wakened by the explosion of a propane tank in the middle of the night. This is the town the ferry leaves from to get us out to our island. It is where we find most of our services: the hardware store, the market, the medical center, the bank, the stationers, restaurants, etc. There is a main street about two blocks long. For several hours we waited for an accurate report. We began imagining special places, in addition to those already mentioned, lost – a unique store that sells household goods, galleries, a marine museum, the just-renovated library – and we were filled with a sense of grief and panic. In the end the lack of wind, the efforts of many surrounding fire companies and a brick wall stopped the spread of a blaze that could have wiped out the whole town. No one was seriously hurt. As it was, a wonderful gallery and its eighty-year-old owner's home above it containing all her own work, an antique store, another gallery and a delicatessen were burned beyond recovery, the fire starting somewhere in the deli. A surgical strike that took out a section of Main Street. These were turn-of-the-last-century clapboard buildings with high ceilings and worn wooden floors. For artists, the loss of their work is something for which no insurance company can compensate them. And only in memory now will live the creak and slap of the deli bakery's front screen door, the ka-chonk of the ancient cash register as you paid for one (or more!) of their delectable glazed crullers drizzled with chocolate – available nowhere else in the world.

Blueberries

This year has been the best anyone to the oldest islander can remember for blueberry picking. It's as if the island itself had won the blueberry lottery, the winnings mounting up over many sparse years. No one knows exactly why. Fewer deer. The right timing of flowering for pollination.

Heavy, persistent rain early in the summer. A good, long-lasting hard frost and lengthy snow cover. Some claim it's natures way of providing plenty for a hard winter in the offing. In any case, the berries are bigger than ever and busting out in clusters. It used to take a powerful lot of picking, berry by berry, to get enough to make a pie. Now only 15 minutes for one picker! (Partly because there are also more mosquitoes this year than ever. Swarms descend on anyone crouching in the field. Every free gift has its price!) Some inveterate pickers feel they have to do this windfall justice and have picked many very large ceramic bread bowls of them. Even many jars of jam do not seem to deplete the supply. Touted for their anti-oxidant abilities, blueberries on a Maine island constitute a form of wealth. Maybe that is why some place "No Picking Please" signs on their property near the road, and others exact the tribute of a pie or cake in exchange for the privilege of picking on their land. I have seen birds drop down in a field and pluck their share. But this bounty could never completely be harvested. This truth keeps some awake at night worrying about how many of those frosty blue babies will drop to the ground never having been tongued and burst against the roof of a mouth, never having caused same mouth to pucker with pleasure from the sweet sourness of the fruit.

Sea Truck

I was on the phone one night when my husband exhorted me to hang it up and come quickly down to the dock. Many others were down there too when I arrived. Taking up the whole space between the town dock and the private dock was what is called a sea truck. It loomed like a truly alien craft. Earlier I had glanced out our window and saw what looked like a very strange vessel coming across the Western Way, some sort of dreadnaught. A quick check with binoculars made me feel it was simply another barge. Not so. It's an amphibious, formerly military vessel used to transport large machinery, which it stows in the maw of its gigantic interior, from island to island. Its tires are ten feet tall! In the almost dark it looked like a crouching dinosaur. There are only a few in the world. And here it was on our shore. It had chosen our harbor as a place to rest for the night, providing us with a memorable island event. Since many of us here have no television, there's no telling what can come to qualify as entertainment.

Coyote

The presence of a coyote has been reported on the island. Some chickens, and more importantly, roosters have disappeared, and some cats. Now, cats are known to light out and get lost in the woods here for long periods of time, and domestic fowl annoy some neighbors to a fair-thee-well, especially when they are allowed to run. So not everyone was ready to believe there was actually a coyote lurking hereabouts. How would a coyote get out here anyway? Swim. Like the deer do. Hmm. One resident, known for leg-pulling, who keeps an assortment of animals off the gravel road we call I-95 – poultry, geese, a pig, sheep, goats – produced a photo he took to "prove" the coyote was real. He had suffered losses at this scoundrel's jaws. A friend, who has no such axes (or teeth) to grind, said she saw the coyote at the end of her driveway once. This I'm more inclined to believe. And belief is the factor here, it seems. Until I actually see the varmint with my own eyes, I'll never be sure of his identity or whether he exists at all. Think of all those legends and myths about the trickster Coyote who is always up to mischief trying to shake things up and catch or *throw* humans off guard to see if we're awake and if we've got the gumption to meet vexation head on.

Memorials

This summer there have been upwards of seven memorial services for people who were members of the year-round or summer communities on our island. This took a toll on everyone. An island by its very geographic isolation forces upon its inhabitants a kind of intimacy and dependence on one another that you cannot avoid or pretend are not crucial to your survival. You get to know your neighbors' habits, their patterns of speech, the things they care about, the way they laugh – or whether they ever do. If you don't want to be *known*, an island isn't the place for you. When anyone dies, there is a rent in the fabric of the community. There are houses where no lights go on anymore. There are holes left that cannot be filled by anyone else. In a city if someone who lives on the same block with you dies, you may never know about it. Here a loss of any kind is *felt*. Everyone is precious and *essential*. A couple of years ago a tree in one of our yards had to be pruned because of some sort of blight. It still lives but it is awkward and unbalanced-looking, and there are what look like sores where limbs were lopped off. It is not itself and neither are we because the artist in her inimitable gait, a kind of languid, rocking strut, no longer goes down to the store carrying her string bag on her arm, wearing her white, wide-brimmed hat, cocked, and one end of a burnt orange shawl thrown over her shoulder; because the composer/pianist, be-haloed by his own pale, thin hirsute curls, no more bends over the keys to bring us into closer alignment with our souls; because the mandolinist will nevermore beam with pleasure as she plucks our heartstrings too and gone are the friends whose keeping of our confidence as something vulnerable and valuable allowed us to move out from under our burdens to grow.

Island Wedding

There are many dimensions to a response a parent might have to her own child's wedding, but I'd like to focus, in this case, on the aspect of its relation to the community. Though we do not live on the island year round, and some would claim we have no right to feel it, we consider this place to be home. So, when our daughter was planning her wedding, it was here she and her husband-to-be, who had also come to love the island, wanted to be married. This community watched her grow from a gangly, bespectacled tomboy into a tall, genuine beauty. They'd observed her temper and triumphs on the tennis court, her painting from ladders the clapboards on our corner. They'd experienced her friendliness beaming from behind the counter when she worked at the store or when they engaged her for babysitting. They'd bought brownies at her lemonade stand and worried with us when, lying on the window seat cushion, she accidentally put her foot through a window and had to be rushed off island for stitching of the long gash on her leg. No secret to them, I'm sure, were her mischiefs, her romantic exploits, or her "experimenting," judgments or commentary on which never reached our ears. They had borne witness to her growing up, her development and had a hand in shaping the person she is coming to be. So, in a year when the island experienced countless losses, and the community needed something to feel hopeful about, many answered our all-island invitation and crowded into the church to attend her wedding. We could scarcely do any of typical wedding chores, but that someone offered, *insisted*, that he or she take that particular task off our hands: luncheon for the wedding party the day of the wedding, dinner the night before, golf carts offered for transport of guests, food for the reception, and on and ON. I lost my own family young. I moved every two years from one setting after another where the inhabitants were anonymous to one another. The feeling our family had that day of being shored up, backed and understood, was without precedent in my experience. It was as real and physical as of a ship being buoyed and borne up by the waves. At a time when feelings of all kinds are whirling – of joy, regret, sorrow, fear, hope, satisfaction and the overpowering electrical current of love, we were held in the embracing matrix of community, so we would not fly apart. The village had helped, had helped us raise this child, so she could enter her dreamed-of life and thrive. Gratitude abounding.

Quiet

It is quieter on the island this summer than it has ever been. For some reason it seems all our hot-rodders have grown up or moved off island. The gunning of unmuffled trucks and three wheelers ramming up and down the island's two mile long main road back and forth, back and forth at too high a speed for civilized folk has been non-existent. There used to be a sense that the island was a pen constraining restless young creatures who longed to have a wide range to roam in. And because they didn't have this range, they paced madly back and forth. They bucked. We shook our heads and furrowed our brows, *Someday someone's going to get hurt!* we warned. Some of us even spoke to the troublemakers. That they are gone is, no doubt, a relief to some – many, perhaps. But something is missing. They were something to complain and become indignant about. Their activities generated a GREAT deal of discussion about what constitutes unacceptable behavior in a community and how to cope with trouble. They provided energy, danger, wildness, youth. They were blatant about something many of us are too proud, too ashamed or afraid to confess: there is something more we all want, and we are angry we don't have it. To say nothing of the fact that there were no jobs here to hold them, so they could stay and one day become citizens who raise an outcry about the too much noise and commotion made by other young people coming up under them.

Crocs

Those clodhopperish, brightly-colored plastic shoes with holes in them have become part of the island uniform along with tee shirts, hats, sweatshirts and vests with our island logo on them. Everywhere you look *down,* someone of any age, either gender, is wearing a pair of them. The first pair I ever saw was on one of my neighbors who is younger and hipper than I am. Hers were orange. I assumed I'd be too old and frumpy for them. Then others started wearing them. When I learned they came in purple and also in a non-holed version, so, when gardening, the dirt wouldn't end up all over your feet, I was sold. Now I have several pair. One for downstairs, one for up. Some I keep for "dress up" – going to island parties or church. Since most of us walk or ride bikes everywhere, they are acceptable in any setting. They can easily be cleaned by hosing them out. And, since I heard from an NPR segment that, compared to other summer shoes – flip-flops and many sandals – they are good for your feet and give sufficient support, I wear them hiking and across the water into town. They are even great for walking on rocks – enough cushion and traction to make it safe and comfortable. At many island doorways you see a many-sized rainbow of them fanned out. Who would have thought in our black/white, neutral toned culture, where coolness over comfort seems to rule, that their color and clunkiness, their good-for-you and not too expensive practicality would be so popular. *Viva les Crocs!*

Blight

Along the main road of our island are many mature maple trees. Typically there are four or five of them lined up in a yard right next to the road. In our yard there are two large-leaved *red* maples. For the last couple of years, their leaves have been curling up and browning before the end of August. This is a new development. Before the leaves curl up and brown, they show terrible-looking black spots about the size of quarters. This looks indeed like a plague. It's official name is black tar spot. A fungus, it is purported to be caused by excessive moisture in the air. Maybe too much fog? But when hasn't there been an excess of that on the Maine coast? About ten years ago great stands of spruces on the island were destroyed by the hemlock looper, a boring insect. Those trees were vulnerable because there had been a drought. We wonder, of course, whether this current blight is connected to global warming. It is not supposed to be harmful to the health of the tree, and no treatment is recommended, but it robs us of our autumn gold. Beauty is essential to the health of souls and the sight of our cringing, bespotted maple leaves causes a kind of grief. Something valuable to our well-being has been lost. To say nothing of how the trees themselves must feel!

Cultural Center

This year on the Fourth of July we had a ribbon-cutting ceremony to open our island cultural center. This day was hard-worked for by many, spearheaded by a really hardworking few. This center houses our museum and has an outdoor café and an all-purpose room upstairs for lectures, classes, movies and art exhibits. That room used to be a dining room in this old building for rusticators who came here early in the last century, until it was moved from the back yard of one of my neighbors and renovated. My favorite part of the museum, and oddly, also a favorite of those who come to the island just for a day, is the wall covered with pictures of islanders who have long ago or recently passed away. It's a way of honoring our regular citizens, of making them dear and a little famous. There are the row of smiling aproned sisters who once owned a restaurant down by the shore known for its lemon pie, and the Swedish artist with the longer-than-Santa Claus's white beard who cooked Christmas dinner for the whole island, complete with glog. There are sea captains, quilters, post and school mistresses, tennis players and boat builders. If there is such a thing as geographic lineage, I feel related to them and proud to be so. When in my city life I tell people I live summers on an island, I see them get a far off, romantic look in their eyes. O, *it must be quiet out there with plenty of time to read.* Hmm. There was so much going on this summer just at the cultural center, it would have been impossible to take it all in and have time for much else: several concerts – classical, jazz, rock, folk – poetry, art, and photography classes, movies twice a week, lectures on the geology of the island, lighthouse keeping, the art of a former resident, etc., *etc.* Yes, of course, you can choose to take time to read – we also have the largest library in the state for a community our size, and it has several special

93

events as well – but there is so much talent here, such a ferment of creative activity, it would be a shame not to partake of some of the prodigious smorgasbord that is offered.

Hermit Thrushes

Not without cause does this bird receive its designated name. Only once, with one of two dear birder friends who visit me here, have I ever seen the hermit thrush "in the feather." And a brilliant rufous feather it is on its back, pronounced dark streaks, as if for lyric emphasis, on its buff-colored breast. It keeps itself deep in the woods as it can, and, sparing as it might be with its physical self-disclosure, it is that much more prodigal with its song. It used to be that only down one lane of the island at dusk, the one I take to visit our beloved cousin, they could be heard. As I walked it seemed that, as in relay, they would pass the melodic baton all down the way, attending me as I walked, censing me with the aroma of their exquisite piccolo-like measures. I imagined they were extolling the properties of the trees and how they point to the fresh prospect the sky can always be counted on to provide. But some years ago I heard them, and at midday, in the island's center, then also at island's end. A happy day was when I could hear one from my home yard at morning. It's as if the thrushes passed the message to each other that this place was safe for those of us who are retiring in nature, but of a passionate, soulful bent. By their presence in greater numbers now, we are decidedly blessed.

Empty Houses

Kitty-corner across the road from us lives a young family, two parents and three children, ages at this writing 12, 9 and 6. They spend about six weeks of the summer here, the father of the family having done so too as a child. While they are here the garage is always open. Sawhorses are set up for the father and grandfather's renovation projects. There is always patch painting going on to keep the cream gold house looking sharp. The kids are playing knights, climbing old apple trees, catching snakes, making art projects. They sell their incredibly creative works at a little stand out front, along with choice pieces of sea glass they've collected and unusual shells and rocks. I bought for seven dollars this summer a bodacious dragon made of scallop and sea urchin shells with green sea glass spikes across his back and nostrils snorting green as well. The kids have humane mesh traps for insects and butterflies that they often come over to show us. Whenever they go by on their bikes they shout out our names in greeting. Their mother sends over bags of cookies, and we trade off sharing meals. At night there might be a Scrabble game going at their house for anyone to join who wants to. When they leave at the end of the summer, the absence is profound. I tear up when I look over there or pass by walking up from or down to the dock. So much mostly joyous activity. Even their squabbles provide the background sounds of life being lived to the full. This is only one example. When I stay a ways into September, as I have this year, and watch the houses on my corner, one by one, go dark, I am struck – and I mean I feel it physically as if I'd been delivered a blow – by the kind of loneliness you can only feel with the departure of those you deeply love.

Storm Surf

This was a summer of near-miss hurricanes. The edges of one strafed the island with heavy rain, finding entries through our clapboards never tried before. Our dinner guests were drenched during the entrée. Some wires came down; some were so frayed, they fried the whole electrical system of friends across the road. The other storm did not affect us directly. It went out to sea, and our shore stayed sunny. But at night the roaring started. Our house is about two miles from the back shore, and the roar sounded like a beast was in our front yard. The next day word got around and, if the island had been a float, it would have sunk, because we were all gathered on one edge of it looking at the waves. One friend who is wheelchair-bound went in front of her backshore house and was almost swept off the rocks that are usually well away from the water. Waves came up over roads, came into the woods, came up over the only landform we have that qualifies as "bluff." On top of it is the chimney, all that's left of a former home, and it was assaulted again and again by surf, what looked like dragon froth, jaw-droppingly high. "Awesome," even in its powerful ancient meaning, is a word that simply cannot do the sight justice. My husband quipped after we had stood with a clutch of others for many minutes of silence, "And we think we have control!" To me it is deeply consoling, danger and all, that there are many ways in which Nature still reigns – indisputably.

Departure Prevention Committee

When I go to the dock to say good-bye to friends and family as they leave at the end of summer, I have joked for the last few years that I am a member of the Departure Prevention Committee and will try to keep them from going. I point out that my efforts have been completely unsuccessful. I'm a total failure in this role, and yet I remain undeterred. No one has ever stayed on because I showed up at the moment they loaded their gear and stepped onto the ferry. I threaten to get shirts with a logo on them of a hand raised in a gesture of "halt" and round up others to put them on and join me. Why do I go through such a silly routine? Probably to distract me and the others from the sadness we might be feeling as we realize it will be, God willing, another year before we see each other again. Too many times that dock has been the place where I last saw someone who had an indelible impact on my life. Island communities are intimate and intense, and the bonds we make here are strong. It is not easy to let dear ones disappear into the fog or get so small as they speed away on the ferry they can't see us still waving and throwing kisses. And who knows, maybe I'll be the one next year who doesn't return. The passage of time, aging, illness, death: these are not plans I like at all. We'll bring this up at the next meeting of the committee and see what we can do about them, what strategies we might employ...

III

Would that [my beloveds] might live a thousand years.
Would there were on this earth no final partings.

– Ariwara Narihira
Tales of Ise

ISLAND GODDESS

It may be rusted
but she's got backbone –
and wings.
Her hair falls in ropes.
Her cockeyed eyes wink
and weep.
Distinctive is
the puncture wound
on her right cheek.
When there's hurt
of any kind,
she swears indignant
blue streaks.
That's why,
periodically,
to protect herself,
her ears shut.
She keeps the animals
close: coyotes, voles.
Her totem
is the hermit thrush,
its quavering melodic phrase.
From what's been shattered,
she takes her jewels.
Her breastplate
bears the insignia
of her place:
the tides and stones,
the clouds and trees.
Crowned by a buoy,
she's got a nose
for beauty, defined
cattywampus-wise.
Don't mess with her
unless you want the love
shaken right out of you.

FINBACK

for RR, CT and AR

We were ready to turn back,
private, hired boatful on a pristine day
30 miles out from Mt. Desert
which lay on the horizon like Ithaca,
farther off than we'd ever seen it:
home, goal, mirage, citadel of huddled rocks.
Oh, but there had been consolations:
a puffin or two, some gannets, shearwaters,
those curious, whiskered snoops, the seals.
There was the lighthouse outpost on
barely-big-as-a-football-field rock, so
storm vulnerable, and salutes to and from
the station's students,
                          but the prize
we were after eluded us, until
someone spotted a circus of harbinger petrels
and rack lines, the upwelling of food,
and there, tucked between waves, the sea's
indigo envelope, a love bolt, the charcoal bulk
of the largest of all, except the blue, animals
with the deepest – resounding through vast
underwater canyons – voice in the world.
Normally boat-shy, it emerged and kept surfacing,
showing, as lover might beloved, its
magnificent length, its whole barnacled self.
Our craft practically capsized as everyone,
even those with seen-it-all means,
shifted in high excitement to the viewing rail.
Nothing enthused friends, who'd been
many times on "watches" prepared me
for this first whale, for the surge of tears, reverential.
How could we label her *leviathan, behemoth, anathema,*
a monster to conquer and kill, this blood sister,
who inspires nothing but
                     drop-on-your-knees-to-the-deck awe?

MORNING

No matter how you feel,
morning comes up beautiful.
You may have passed the night
wracked and grappling with if
you'll last after the death
of what you cherished most,
but the light, first appearing as
a rosy nimbus over your world,
fingers, like the seeker of fine goods,
everything with its attention.
It casts shafts of approbation
on a stand of spruces, on black bags
of trash chucked by the side of the road.
It throws the shadow of your house
over that of your neighbor
illumining just the roof line
and its encrustments of golden lichen.
It bejewels while it consumes the dew
on the heads of the grasses and polishes
to a high turquoise gloss the water
over which the body of the white gull,
bright in its pinions, wings
like the hope of certain salvation.
Does it not care what you've lost,
how you tossed and sobbed, that dawn
finds you wretched and shaking?
Can it only drape you in a mantle of warmth
and fold you into a new day?

WILD CRANBERRIES

The week we conceded
the hope for gold,
we came upon a trove of them
at one horn of the cove
low and creeping
among a collage of cones
lichen, moss and crumpled leaves
beneath tall, needled trees
of night-dark green.
They were red as the No!
to summer's end,
as the woodchopper's
January nose,
wee as crimson petit peas
and each a globe of its own
variations on rose,
their surfaces burnished
individually.
We gathered them
in a cobalt bowl
then boiled them to a froth
to a pink for sauce
to sweeten and sharpen
our daily portion:
for our meats, our defeats,
a relish
of fluid rubies.

THE LAST

We wore the same size and loved the same colors:
purple and deep blue, especially in flowers.
I filled her planters with them later
which she appreciated with a face-pleating smile.
Twenty years apart in age, from very different
backgrounds, yet both secular: heathen, Jewish,
we shared that early catastrophic losses
had summoned forth from us hidden strengths.
She suggested we walk together to the island's
farthest point. Always eager to greet the world,
she took these miles, not the easiest of terrains,
with her slow, forward-leaning gait, enjoying
grasses, lichens, shore birds, the horizon
drawing nearer in the fog. She had albums full
of images like these she'd snapped and savored
and you might receive the most flattering photo of yourself
she'd taken without your knowing it in the mail.

We stepped into the frame of a new house being built.
It was there she chose to tell me
that her blood was slowly going white.
Not to worry, there would be more time.
There was. We hugged. We teared up. Cancer,
mine, hers, brought us closer, but we were never able
again to take that or any other walk.
In ceramics class she made earrings for me
and other friends. She knew, really knew
she was loved and was considerate enough
to understand we would want mementos.
Ferocity she reserved for self critique
for deploring hurt-dealing evils.
Days after she died just her voice came to me in a dream
clear as if I'd been struck awake by a bell.
She was so sorry she couldn't be there when I called.

in memory of Bea Weinreich

WALKING WITH BETSY

How are you doing? she asks, as we set out,
and, a minute later, question, the same.
How is she? *Taking each day, just
taking each day* – quavering smile.

Aren't the trees beautiful? she marvels,
as if she'd never seen trees before.
We pass under spruce and tamarack branches
down to the shore. She asks
about my daughters, my writing
showing she still knows who I am.
She wants to pick a stone for taking back
to remind her of this place it's so good to be.
*It's been quieter on the island this summer,
so much quieter,* she says again, then again.
She reaches for a rock striated with olive
and gray that matches her sweater and pants.

She's gone with me, her spirit's lantern
fearless and bright into corners otherwise too dark,
hearing pain no one else could understand.
How can I stay by her as she drifts
like a ship off its moorings out to sea?
She puts the stone she's cradled and caressed
saying, *I love you*, into my hands,
the face of it marked and outlined, as if
for emphasis, as if dropped in water
rippling outward, by the shape of a tear.

*In loving memory
Elizabeth Granlund Wells*

WINTERSPEAK

My friend is dying. She always said now
was the most beautiful season of the year here.
To see her, first time on the island for me,
                                            this tide.
The water is knife-blade gray – carbon steel.
Waves slam and crash as if
          they could break the fact of the rocks.
On the dock wind would tear the wimpling,
stretched-to-its-limits flag right off
the post office pole. White caps
raise their Hydra heads. Lights from the few
inhabited homes throw halos onto the
higher-than-humans drifts. When she speaks,
not with her mouth anymore, but with
          dark, deep-set eyes and a face creased
from being pressed too fast against death,
that wordless speech is keen, penetrating,
                                            wonderstruck.
It vibrates deep in my chest.
When she sleeps, too many seconds
          elapse between breaths.
Lines she requested I read her
go slack as windless jibs. More snow
sifts down at dusk, fine and gray
as last grains left us through the glass.

In loving memory
Robin Richman (1944-2009)

ELEGY FOR ROBIN

You've just died and I can't bear
hearing you spoken of in the past tense.
Your death is nigh unto impossible to accept.
Not so you, who, when shown the image of your tumor,
smiled, fascinated by its many tentacles.
Walking with your spare frame always tilted forward,
you emptied yourself wholly into moments,
pushing up the sleeves of one your ancient
wool sweaters, combing with your fingers
shocks every shade of gray and gesticulating
passionately about almost everything.
Even at the end, your eyes burned with wide blue irony.

When I arrived and departed from the island,
you insisted I sit on the ferry or in your truck
while you unloaded my 20+ pieces of baggage
by yourself. When *I* was sick – no small task! –
you planted my garden. When you asked
what you could do for the wedding and I said
we needed dill for the crab dip, you brought *sheafs*
of perfect, pungent green. And when the dog
you gave us, sweetest pup of the litter, sweetest
I ever knew, got run over, you drove home and back
with a bolt of finest silk to wrap her in for burial.
When, tearful, I thanked you, your speech gone,
for all this and more, you shrugged as if to say,
Once in the realm of love, what else does one do?
What shroud could be fit raiment for your ascent?
I would tug at it and unwind you well again. Well.

GHOST OVERWHELM

So many are no longer here,
so many I loved.
My rooms are overfull of ghosts.
I can't get past them.
They crowd me out.
They hide behind doors,
surprise me looking up baleful
from the bottom of my coffee mug.
One of them will plop onto my lap
and I'll have to embrace him.
More tears, more tears!
as my arms close again
upon air. Soon, I fear,
there will be nothing left of me.
Of course there won't!
There'd better be some relief
in joining them...
Is it better to be haunted
than to be completely bereft?

ROBIN

Every nestling is the world reborn.

Friend with the burnt orange breast,
black head, gray back, run-stopping
across the lawn, nipping up worms
and grubs I'd never in my life
be able to spot, thank you for lodging near,
for choosing the ledge under my deck
for a nestsite. Your company
during this time of loss
is anything but common.

So many of your ilk are, and ought to be,
afraid of us. And you fly off the nest
most times I open the back door
till I'm safely out of range. But
I couldn't resist borrowing a ladder
to climb up, and, careful not to touch,
look down into your expertly
turned out sanctum, intricate weavings
of twigs and tufts, whorled as a galaxy,
including a strand of plastic pink cord.

Too late for the heaven-hued eggs,
but not for the speckle-feathered mass
and tiny golden nestling mouths
opening upward. Maybe we haven't –
yet – completely broken the continuum.
Hope pecks through my dejected shell.

HELD, HEALING

Hosea 11:3-4

How is it that tonight
out on the calm summer
star-sparged water
with friends in their boat
I, who can look at the night sky
terrified of the infinite,
of falling and falling at the end
into blackness, into vacuum
without bottom,
look up at the Milky Way
never this clear
from light-polluted land
and think of the phrase,
"bands of love," that I feel
fed, as we ride, by
the Mother of the universe,
her milk, and lifted
to the dark cheek of heaven?

for Dan and Cindy Rome

JACK'S FACES

from the paintings of John Heliker

At first it was irksome to view
one of his paintings of figures
gathered around a table
or a single soul standing on a shore:
all the faces were blurred or veiled,
it seemed, their features indistinct.
The line of a jaw, nose shapes, brows
only hinted at. Who could these people be?
Anyone we know? One of us? Ourselves?
Ghost faces, they floated onto the present
canvas, sketchy as our memories or dreams.
Their images the ones the mind plucks
out of time and all encounters to keep.
Was his vision so compelling, he couldn't
actually see anyone else as they were?
No, is what we began, over time, to feel.
No, he did not presume to know
another well enough to fill in all details.
His portrayals do not limit them
to his interpretation of who they are or were,
making high resolution portraits by others
seem almost violate. His subjects'
bodies have a carriage of such relaxed dignity,
they imply his attitude toward all to be
simply and only respect. Even his self-portraits,
though clearer, more recognizable, are still
blear. A mystery, bottomless, we are
largely unknown, even to ourselves.
Our faces are like rubbings of open-eyed
funereal masks, expressions mild.
When set as individuals within
our common scenes and rooms,

maybe Jack, through his pale pigments, wondered
as he passed among us, if we don't all blend
into one shifting visage, a spirit self
we're living into, ultimate, eternal?

NEIGHBORS

When I leave the cellar light on,
Isabel always chides me.
Sometimes I leave it on purposely
for her as a joke, but she says
at least there was *one* light
in her sleepless vigil!
In the dark, she names to herself
the owners and former owners
of each house in order down the road.
She repeats stories about them.
About how old Eber wanted a tour
of the harbor on his way to the hospital,
how he knew it was his last chance
to soak up the view alive.
When I came home after surgery,
she was there with fish chowder, warm bread
she mixes until *the beaters go wild*
dancing on top of the dough,
her garden's greens and flowers, rhubarb pie.
Cottage cheese cartons of her strawberries
appear on our kitchen table, but whenever
I bring over a simple plate of cookies
she exclaims, *You'll spoil us!*

Days rain is a question, I wait
to see if Stan hangs out their wash.
If he does, I do. He's never been wrong.
Grass is never allowed much growth.
He mounts his riding throne and mows
heraldic patterns in their considerable lawn.
I can't believe there's anything left to fix
over there, but every morning their
cellar door stands at attention, open.
He's down at his workbench puttering.
If you need a certain nut or screw,

a ladder, any tool, he's got it and freely
lends his hand as well. We'd never
installed a light fixture. We were sweating.
He stood and watched, kibitzing a little.
Never touched a thing. *See!* He knew
we could do it if we tried. I'm pushing
a cartful of luggage up the hill.
Ya know, Sam, it's easier if you go
the other way. Next time,
he meets me at the dock with his vehicle.

Stiffer, eighty plus and slower now,
they walk down several times a day
end of season to see everyone of all ages off.
Next year, next year they say with smiles and hugs.
Once I'm on the boat, spotting a tear in my eye,
Stan shouts down with a laugh. *Don't worry!*
You'll make it! Not without you, I reply.

For Stan and Isabel Seimer

REQUEST ON DANCING ROCKS
Baker's Island

No dance I could ever
have managed on these granite slabs
tumbled and jutting
from one of this continent's
last abandoned outpost islands
could begin to match the slam and crash,
the thunder, the sundering
of waves from the vastness
battering this rock, wanting it to give
wanting to have an effect.
Patient sea and passionate –
the roar, the sob and swoon –
eons to wear anything so hard
smooth and blunt.
At the end to be transmuted,
to stroke, to chrism these big pink stones
as a liquid element, to cover them
snug as translucent, transitory silk,
to draw back, to gather forth
and throw myself solely
into being broken, being dashed
in loving, purely loving, the earth

LARCHES

are my favorite trees on this island.
They're not stately like the spruces,
not complacent as shady old maples.
Not too proud to express themselves,
their candles are *out there*
shooting every which way like
hands on a kid's stick figure, or,
in the same picture, rays around the sun.
They're spikes of hair on someone
just waking, saying, happy to be up
and in the world, to be here growing
in muck, getting tall, getting tough enough
to push farther north than any tree on this continent.
Yet their pale, silvergreen needles, which,
unlike those of most conifers, turn
bright yellow and drop off in autumn,
are soft, almost like fur. You can
pull your fingers along a branch
as you would up a cat's tail.
It's soothing, like their sap on wounds.
Spindly, spidery, gangly, gawky, feathered,
alias tamarack, alias hackmatack, they've
been boat floaters, railroad pavers, telegraph poles.
Funky, they could get down.
Don't-know-any-better tree,
making your comeback,
stay strong against pests,
stay up.

for Carolyn Brunelle

PLENILUNE, AUGUST

Tonight as you rose, fulsome fruit,
unearthly over the sea,
luminous, looming,
we stopped our talk. We set down
our goblets and forks, our politics,
the formulation of our next gay rejoinder.
Sheening the waves into which you permitted
your perfect sphere to be smithereened,
you spilled at our feet
all the coin of your realm.
Speechless for some moments we remained,
relieved that we could still
be brought to silence
by something so great big and beautiful.
Votaries then, we would take and feed
on your scintillant slivers
to be silvered within.
We would follow the path you extend,
its invitation to join in the fleet-footed reel
of light rioting, light brightening
the deep, the darknesss.

NIGHT OF ELEMENTS DISGUISED

The scars shone frightfully in the sky
where, out of reach, hung the silver boon.
Shivers ran all the way to the sea
where muttering staves crashed on the strand.
A rare word flitted from tree to tree
and needs ruffled the leaves and crooned.

for Bill Goldberg

THRUMCAP

Named for the snug, warm
weather-anything seaman's hats
made from wool's weft ends,
this out-jutting knob, the island's
very tip takes some getting to,
but can be reached over a long,
prohibitive-even-to-SUV's
rock causeway ruched
with kelp's maroon, crunchy
under boot. From here, beauty
every degree round: like combers below them
writ large – Acadia's mountains,
the outer islands – creatures furred with spruce,
cove crescents, the Pool, the treacherous Gut,
the open ocean – dance floor of the sun.
It's an outcrop over-poured with deep yellow
Xanthoria lichen, never present unless
the air is Eden clean. Five stars
in the all-species secret guidebook.
To be on this anointed spot
with a breeze running its fingers
through your locks, and quivering weeds
tough enough to seed in cracks
is to be laved all through with an amber wash,
to be lavished as one never expecting
to be elect with the world's superlatives:
oil, honey, topaz – gold and to be relieved
there's still a place for earth to breathe
and to be – just itself.

DEADHEADING

Such a crass, even brutal expression!
Nevertheless, I'm obsessed
at this point in the summer
near its – God forbid! – end,
ruthless for further flowering.
I snip off the dry, spent blossoms
to encourage stems to extend
color's bright and delicate term.
It's an axiom: the more a plant
is cut back, the more it blooms.

If I applied this to my life,
would I be so quick to clip away
scions that don't produce,
just lop off branches of skills,
friendships, interests no longer of use
and not pretend that wizened sticks
may someday once again give forth
green? I have shelves displaying
the husks of what was once dear.
My house is a museum of who I've been.

Then there's the sense of terror
when I contemplate a surge of growth,
everything out, nothing withheld,
all my petals unpeeled, to the elements,
to bees. How could I sustain,
withstand, support the life force pouring
untrammeled through my vacuoles,
the unmitigated thrill?

SAX

for GW

Hey, brother, we listening
wish we were your instrument.
We wish you'd hold us up close,
put your lips to our reedy piece
and blow down through us
curve and bell.
Press our valves.
We'd like to feel your finger pads
hot on our cool metal.
Riff any way you please
with us – improvise
on our motifs.
Let our stops out.
We want to feel the flow of your notes
through our vessels, down to
the tiniest little veins,
the curl and interskirl –
elaborations, winding
and twining like vines
springing with leaves.
Play us sultry
as an August night in the Keys;
let us whine.
Play us sweet.
Let your tune croon us
out of our old hides
into weeping,
weeping our blues free.
Play in us lines
that fly and fly before
they dive and dig,
dig in down and deep –
plow,
then climb, scaling our peaks.
Brother, let us breathe
your music, release us
from speech.

120

WHERE HAS SUMMER GONE?

for Polly Bunker at the Whale's Rib

Why it weren't but yesterday
I set them begonias out.
People ask how they get
so full o' blossoms. I say
I guess they just got excited!
A whole power load of customers
just came right in. How they do
take on when they see all I got:
Arlene's quilts, them funny little
rings that light up when you press 'em.
Picked me clean! I'm all in.
Wish to goodness I had some o' those
smoked mussels. I could eat 'em
can and all! Nothing left much
but one o' these shirts. They couldn't
***believe,** ye-us, I designed 'em myself:*
the swoop of dolphins and the little
*different color fish, **surprisin'** on the back.*
Aren't those cunnin' bars of soap
shaped like rocks? About now
I get to missin' Tud.
He'd scythe the brush out back.
Anybody use a scythe any more?
I get such a lonely feeling, winter
comin' on. I see those empty houses . . .
*Oh! **where** has the summer gone?*
Passed us right by! Did we have any sun?
No sooner warm than it commences
fog. I do have one wool sweater left
Eva knit. Might be your size,
Seems as though it's your color. Try it on.
"Dressin' room's" just that space over there
behind the door! And, why don't you

just **take** these earrings. Here, I'll wrap 'em
in this lavender paper. How they do
sparkle! Just take 'em. No charge.
Every little ache, I wonder,
Is that the cancer again?
My poppies are all but done.

DARK HOUSES

The houses stand empty at summer's end
We will always have to leave each other
There is no togetherness in death

Such good company we have on this corner!
Uproarious card games, feasts, walks, deep talks, porch chats
Then, since we can't live here all year, overmany good-byes

Why should we even get attached? A terrible
stab-to-the-heart sadness shoots through me
Houses once full of friends stare back at me blankly

I peer in for evidence they've been present:
An unfolded afghan, that last glass in the drainer,
A forgotten potted plant, sails draped askew over a rafter

The sun casts its slow searchlight crosshatched over their floors.
Will we ever see each other again? Who's next to die?
Once screen doors' constant creak and slap. Now silence.

In the quiet, bolts of loneliness strike.
How can I withstand them? Only by looking at the sky,
the movement of clouds, the play of light on water

Only by listening to the knowing wind moan, trees shuddering
The houses are dark under less of a moon
We will always have to leave each other.

SEPTEMBER LIGHT

No longer the white, high overhead
down-bearing blast. Slanted now,
it casts the whole about-to-go show
in gold, licking the taken-for-granted
grasses to a flaxen fare-thee-well.
Draping even the deepest green boughs
in golden shawls, whetting waters
to an excruciating blue, cleansing the air
with astringent chill, it illumines, near the end,
what a treasure, unsurpassed, it's all along been:
tansy's yellow tabs, apple's red, its bulge,
crow caw, windlift, cricket, cricket.

for Roger Lipsey

MOONLESS NIGHTS

I'm alone on my corner,
my neighbors flown to their winter roosts,
when Jupiter makes his point against the night
and the Milky Way, made bold by the dark,
unties the long white sashes of its robe,
when, despite a few blinking satellites,
it's quiet as it gets in this engined world,
I hear the buoy bell as a call to thought
and waves lapping softly in the cove
as if the tired earth were lying, beloved,
by my side, sighing, sighing.

GREAT HEAD, DUSK, OCTOBER

This is the ground I'll be scattered on,
this knoll barricaded with rock
that juts into the Western Way.
From here I survey the last point,
its now black evergreen teeth
sawing fog
that spumes off distant mountains
from locomotive waves,
dull bright as coffin metal.
Over me, dark, low underclouds
prowl, extending, withdrawing
their filamentous claws.
Ethereal, cinereal, they're
rolling out toward night,
toward cold, the ocean beyond,
a cortege
shadowing unrelieved horizon.
Already my spirit follows.

What joy in having been at all,
in feeding the fire and knowing
everything isn't about us.

– Brendan Galvin
"A Cold Bell Ringing in the East"

Susan Deborah (Sam) King is a writer, teacher and leader of groups on creativity and spirituality. Her previous book about Maine was *Tabernacle: Poems of an Island*. This is her fourth book of poems. She lives in Minneapolis and on an island off the Maine coast. Her website is www.susandeborahking.com